Alexander Berkman

ABC OF
ANARCHISM

ABC
OF ANARCHISM

Alexander Berkman

FREEDOM PRESS
LONDON

First published in USA by the Vanguard Press, 1929
Second American edition by the Freie Arbeiter Stimme, 1936

First English edition by Freedom Press, May 1942
Reprinted November 1942
Second English edition November 1945
Third English edition March 1964
Reprinted 1968, 1971, 1977, 1980, 1984, 1987, 1992, 1995, 2000, 2006

Freedom Press
84b Whitechapel High Street
London E1 7QX

ISBN 0 900384 03 4

Publisher's Note
Berkman's original work was issued in America in 1929 under the title *What is Communist Anarchism?* It contained three parts headed 'Now', 'Anarchism' and 'The Social Revolution'. The book was reissued in 1936 by the Freie Arbeiter Stimme in New York with a new title *Now and After: The ABC of Communist Anarchism*. The present edition contains parts two and three of the original work: on grounds of expense, part one has been omitted. The text is otherwise that of the 1929 edition. A short biographical sketch of the author has been added.

Design and DTP by Jayne Clementson

Printed in Great Britain by Aldgate Press
Units 5/6 Gunthorpe Workshops, Gunthorpe Street, London E1 7RQ

CONTENTS

ALEXANDER BERKMAN:

AN INTRODUCTION

The *ABC of Anarchism* was first published in 1929, by the Vanguard Press of New York, under the title *What is Communist Anarchism?* It comprised three parts: 'Now', 'Anarchism', and 'The Social Revolution'. It was re-issued in 1936, by *Freie Arbeiter Stimme* of New York, with the new title of *Now and After: The ABC of Communist Anarchism*. It was first published in Britain, this time as *ABC of Anarchism*, in May 1942, by Freedom Press, but without part one. Altogether, it has been reprinted five times by the present publishers. This edition remains exactly the same as previous editions, despite obvious 'dating' of some words and phrases. The *ABC of Anarchism* is now an historic document. Indeed, George Woodcock has called it a minor classic of libertarian literature. That, however, is not the reason for its republication. The reason is that it still remains one of the best introductions to the ideas of anarchism, written from the communist-anarchist viewpoint, in the English language. Its author, Alexander Berkman, was no mere theoretician or 'intellectual'. He had been a militant activist for much of his life.

★   ★   ★

Alexander Berkman was born in November, 1870, at Wilno (Vilnius), Lithuania, which was then in part of the Imperial Russian Empire, had been the capital of the old Duchy of Lithuania and later just within the borders of the Lithuanian Soviet 'Socialist' Republic. At the time that

Alexander Berkman was born, Russia was going through one of its blackest periods of reaction. Moreover, there had been a significant change within the anti-Tsarist and revolutionary movement. The largely aristocratic Nihilists, who spent most of their time agitating among the peasants, had become increasingly disillusioned. Activity became more concentrated on the towns and cities. The 1870s also saw the rise of terrorism against Tsarism and its officials. More workers and artisans, some of whom were Jewish, became involved. By 1880, the Tsar had assumed almost total power, and many thousands of revolutionaries had been hanged, jailed or banished to Siberia. Young Alexander was strongly influenced by the idealism and self-sacrifice of the revolutionaries' struggles, not least by those of his uncle Maxim, who was exiled to Siberia. By the time he was fifteen, Berkman joined a group engaged in the study of revolutionary writings – itself a treasonable activity. He was expelled from school, and was given what was called a 'wolf's passport', which in effect closed almost all professions or trades to him. At sixteen, he was compelled to leave Russia. Alexander Berkman arrived in the United States early in 1888. America, however, was not the paradise that so many immigrants and would-be immigrants expected it to be.

In 1882 the German advocate of revolutionary violence, Johann Most, arrived in New York. He immediately began a speaking tour in all American cities where anarchist and revolutionary socialist groups existed. Of all American cities, Chicago was the most fertile for revolutionary propaganda. In 1883 that city could claim at least 3,000 anarchists, with one German language daily, two German weeklies, a Bohemian weekly and an English fortnightly. A Central Labour Union was founded in 1883, and by 1886 was largely supported by the organised workers in the city. The demand for an Eight-Hour day began in the spring, and by the beginning of May almost 70,000 workers were either on strike or had been locked out by their employers. At the centre of the struggle was the McCormick Harvester Works, which had locked out its men and hired scabs and blacklegs – with 300 Pinkerton gunmen to protect them. Meetings were regularly broken up by the police, and on 3rd May they opened fire on the crowd and killed a number of people. Next day, a protest meeting was held in Haymarket Square, but as it began raining and the crowd was drifting away 200 police marched into the square. At that moment a bomb was thrown towards the police from a side street. The police started firing into the crowd – and at each other! – and a few of the crowd shot back at the police. Seven cops were killed or died later, and between 20 and 30 workers were also killed by the police. Following the incident, many Chicago anarchists were rounded-up and eight prominent revolutionaries, including Parsons and Spies, were put on trial for murder. The prosecution, however, never attempted to prove that any of them had thrown the bomb. They just concentrated on their anarchist beliefs and the violent statements of some of them. Seven were condemned to death; and on 11th November 1887, four of them were hanged. The others were jailed and, some years later, after an inquiry had looked into the case and found no evidence that any of the accused anarchists were involved, they were released. Parsons, Spies and their two comrades had been judicially murdered by the State. The young Berkman arrived in America a few months after.

Under the influence of Johann Most, Alexander Berkman soon joined the revolutionary anarchist movement, first in the Yiddish-speaking group, the Pioneers of Liberty. He also became friendly with another dynamic anarchist, Emma Goldman, who had arrived in the United States just after the Chicago tragedy. Later, they became lovers. But it was the Homestead Steel strike which really aroused Berkman to action. Emma Goldman describes the terrible sequence of events thus:

"It was in the year 1892, at the time of the Homestead Steel strike – the first and greatest life-and-death struggle of the steelworkers of the State of Pennsylvania against their feudal lord, Andrew Carnegie. It aroused the whole country to the slavery and exploitation in the steel industry. That great struggle, powerfully described by Alexander Berkman in his Prison Memoirs, was accompanied by the importation of Pinkerton thugs (the favourite detective and police defenders of the American plutocracy of fifty years ago) who killed eleven strikers, among them a child of ten. The person responsible for that crime was Henry C. Frick, the representative and

business partner of Carnegie. The brutal attitude of Frick towards the
strikers, his public declaration that he would rather see every striker killed
than concede a single demand, and the final murder on 6th July 1892 of
eleven unarmed working-men, roused America to indignation. Even the
conservative press denounced Frick in the sharpest terms. Throughout
America, the workers gave vent to their feelings in protest meetings. But
there was only one man who translated the wrath of the toilers into a heroic
act. That man was Alexander Berkman. On 22nd July 1892, he entered the
office of H.C. Frick and attempted his life. Three bullets lodged in Frick's
body, but he survived. Berkman received a prison sentence of 22 years,
although his act – according to the laws of the State of Pennsylvania – called
for only seven years. To give our comrade such a cruel sentence, six charges
were framed up against him: because he dared to strike at the very heart of
the American industrial plutocracy."

Emma Goldman omits to mention that she also assisted in the
preparation of the assassination attempt on Frick. Alexander Berkman
actually spent fourteen years in the Allegheny Penitentiary in Pennsylvania,
of which over twelve months were in solitary confinement. Richard
Drinnon comments that his capacity to resist the authorities' attempts to
break his will was nothing short of heroic. After his release, Berkman wrote
his famous *Prison Memoirs of An Anarchist*. He then, once again, threw
himself into the revolutionary struggle. He began lecture tours, and helped
organise the free, Ferrer, school in New York. He was one of its first
teachers.

*   *   *

At one time, Berkman edited, with Emma Goldman, the anarchist monthly,
Mother Earth. In 1914, the so-called Great War broke out in Europe. In the
United States, Berkman began an anti-militarist campaign which soon
spread throughout the American continent. Together with Emma
Goldman, he founded the No Conscription League. In 1915, he moved to
San Francisco, where he started the anarchist paper, *Blast*, which continued
until July 1916. Soon after the outbreak of the war in Europe, a number of
'socialist' and 'anarchist' renegades blamed Germany for starting the war,

and came out in support of the Entente. But the vast majority of anarchists, including Goldman, Malatesta, Faure, Rocker and Berkman remained true to their internationalist and anti-militarist principles. Berkman saw the war as a capitalist struggle for profit, trade routes and power with the masses serving as cannon fodder. Nevertheless America entered that struggle in 1916; and during a Preparedness Parade a bomb was thrown. The anarchist militants, Mooney and Billings, were framed. The now-super-patriotic 'socialists' and labourites refused to have anything to do with the matter, and left them to their fate – but not the anarchists. Berkman organised meetings in their defence all over the States, but to no avail. Berkman's anti-war and anti-conscription campaign, however, was beginning to worry the authorities: it was recognised as a serious danger. Berkman and Goldman would have to be taught a lesson! By 1917, the No Conscription League was suppressed. Alexander Berkman, Emma Goldman and many other anarchists were arrested in New York. Alexander and Emma both got two years' imprisonment, a 10,000-dollars' fine and deportation on release. At the same time, the San Francisco authorities indicted Berkman for alleged complicity in the Preparedness bombing. The New York authorities intended to hand him over to San Francisco. But they, and the Federal Government in Washington, had second thoughts. The Trade Unions sent various delegations to the Governor of the State of New York to protest against his extradition to California, but, even more important, anarchist workers in Petrograd and the sailors at Kronstadt organised large demonstrations and threatened the life of the American Ambassador to Russia. The American Government took fright, and Berkman served his two years in Atlanta jail, Georgia, of which seven months were in solitary. Moreover Berkman informed the notorious J. Edgar Hoover that, whatever the laws might be, he would follow the dictates of his conscience. On release, Berkman and Emma Goldman were deported and, at the end of December 1919, arrived in Russia. They were welcomed as heroes. But all was not well in 'Soviet' Russia.

In March 1917, revolution broke out in Russia. It was a popular revolt in which soldiers who were ordered out against the workers and peasants sided with them. There were mutinies at the Front, and hundreds of thousands deserted the army and made their way homewards. Throughout the summer, workers took control of their factories and the peasants expropriated the landowners. The liberal labour government, first of Prince Lvov and then of Alexander Kerensky, attempted to continue the war. By October (November), the government had become completely discredited. Furthermore, the Bolsheviks, or Communists as they called themselves after 1918, had got control of a number of key Soviets, and in particular the Petrograd Soviet. On 25th October (7th November by the new calendar), the Bolshevik-controlled Revolutionary Committee of the Petrograd Soviet staged a *coup d'etat* in the capital. This was followed by *coups* in Moscow and elsewhere. The Bolsheviks established a Council of People's Commissars. They had become the government! The anarchists had supported, and where at liberty had taken part in, the first revolution. They had also advocated and taken part in the expropriation of the landowners, and in the takeovers of factories. Members of the Moscow Anarchist Federation had also participated in the October insurrection in that city; but the anarchists did not support the Bolsheviks when they formed a government. Relations between the anarchists and the Bolsheviks soon became strained. Within months, anarchists and social revolutionaries were being arrested and sometimes shot by the *Cheka* – the Communist 'secret' police. Following the Treaty of Brest Litovsk, and the subsequent intervention by the imperialist powers, some anarchists gave conditional support to the regime, and some even joined the Red Army. But relations between the Bolsheviks on the one hand and the anarchists and social revolutionaries on the other went from bad to worse. In the Ukraine, Nestor Makhno and his partisan army were engaged in battle, first with the Austro-Germans, then the White armies of Denikin and, after a very shaky agreement with the Red Army, with the Bolsheviks themselves. Production, both in industry and agriculture, was almost at a standstill and millions were dying of starvation. This was the situation that Alexander Berkman and Emma Goldman found when they arrived. Though an opponent of government and the state, Berkman – mainly owing to his lack of knowledge of the situation – was rather more sympathetic towards the Bolsheviks than those anarchists who had been in the revolution and in Russia during the first two years of Communist rule. He was, of course, opposed to the interventionists and the Whites. At first, he and Emma Goldman tried to work with the Bolsheviks. They soon found this was impossible.

⋆   ⋆   ⋆

Bolshevik harassment of the anarchists had been mounting ever since the *Cheka* launched its first raids against the Moscow Federation in April 1918. By the summer of 1920, thousands of anarchists, Mensheviks and social revolutionaries were in prison, concentration camps or exile in Siberia. And during the summer, both Emma Goldman and Berkman vehemently protested at the harassment of their comrades to the Second Congress of the Communist International, then meeting in Moscow. Lenin attempted to reassure them by asserting that no anarchists would be persecuted for their beliefs and that only 'bandits' and Makhno's anarchist insurrectionists were being suppressed. But the final crunch came early in 1921. The White armies of Kolchak, Denikin and Wrangle, together with the interventionists, had all been defeated. The Bolsheviks had concluded an armistice with Poland, and the Menshevik government of Georgia had been put to flight by the Red Army. But throughout 1920, there had been numerous peasant rebellions. By February 1921, after the government had announced that the very meagre bread ration was to be cut by a third, strikes and spontaneous meetings broke out in Petrograd and Moscow. The government attempted to break the strikes by concentrating large numbers of troops in Petrograd, and by denying the workers their rations if they did not go back to work. The situation was being watched by the sailors of the Baltic Fleet stationed at the naval base of Kronstadt. On 24th February, they rebelled and demanded the re-introduction of free Soviets, freedom of speech and press to all workers, peasants, anarchists and left socialists. The Bolshevik government – and particularly Trotsky and Zinoviev – replied by bombarding the naval base and then attacking it with units of the Red Army and the *Cheka*. Emma Goldman, Berkman and Perkus, the secretary of the Russian Workers' Union of the United States, tried to mediate. The statement which they sent to President Zinoviev was deliberately conciliatory. They wrote:

"To keep silent now is impossible and even criminal. The events which have just occurred oblige us as anarchists to speak frankly and set forth our attitude towards the present situation.

"The spirit of discontent and unrest among the workers and sailors is the result of facts which require the most serious attention. Cold and hunger have given rise to discontent; the absence of the least possibility of discussion and criticism has forced the workers and sailors to declare their grievances formally.

"The White-Guardist bands would like to and could exploit this discontent for their own interests. Hiding behind the sailors, they call for the Constituent Assembly, free trading and other similar advantages. We anarchists have long exposed the fundamental error in these demands, and we declare before everyone that we will fight, arms in hand, against any counter-revolutionary attempt, together with all the friends of the Social Revolution, and even at the side of the Bolsheviks.

"We are of the opinion that the conflict between the Soviet government and the workers and sailors should be liquidated, not by arms, but by means of a revolutionary, fraternal, agreement in a spirit of comradeship. For the Soviet government to have to recourse to bloodshed in the present situation will neither intimidate nor pacify the workers; on the contrary, it will only serve to increase the crisis and reinforce the work of the Allies and the counter-revolutionaries.

"What is more important, the use of force by the Workers and Peasants Government against the workers and peasants will provoke a disastrous repercussion on the international revolutionary movement. It will result in incalculable injury to the Social Revolution. Comrade Bolsheviks, reflect before it is too late! You are about to take a decisive step.

"We submit to you the following proposal: to elect a commission of five members including anarchists. This commission will go to Kronstadt to resolve the conflict by peaceful means. In the present situation, it is the most radical solution. It will have international revolutionary importance."

Unfortunately for Berkman, the Bolsheviks ignored his plea. Looking back in retrospect, perhaps he and Emma were being just a little too naive, and too conciliatory. Lenin, Trotsky and Zinoviev were all tough politicians who had no intention of losing power if they could help it. Berkman, on the other hand, was, in the words of Victor Serge, a representative of an idealistic generation that had completely vanished in Russia. Berkman, he said, manifested an inner tension that sprang from the idealism of his youth; but when his tension relaxed he became dejected. On 7th March, a full-scale artillery duel was under way. "Days of anguish and cannonading," he wrote in his diary. "My heart is numb with despair; something has died within me. The people on the street look bowed with grief, bewildered. No one trusts himself to speak. The thunder of heavy guns rends the air." The suppression of Kronstadt had a shattering effect on Berkman. And he wandered helplessly through the streets of Petrograd. The Russian anarchists made one last attempt to alert the world in general and the international labour movement in particular to the situation in Soviet Russia. Alexander Berkman and Emma Goldman added their names to a statement by the League of Anarchist Propaganda, the Anarcho-syndicalist League (Golos Truda) and the Russian Confederation of Anarcho-syndicalists, which was sent to Lenin, the Communist Party, the Communist International, the All-Russian Central Council of Trade Unions and other organisations, in July 1921. It was a lengthy document enumerating the persecution of anarchists by the Bolshevik government. This also had no effect.

"Grey are the passing days," Berkman noted in his diary. "One by one the embers of hope have died out. Terror and despotism have crushed the life born in October. The slogans of the Revolution are forsworn, its ideals stifled in the blood of the people. The breath of yesterday is dooming millions to death; the shadow of today hangs like a black pall over the country. Dictatorship is trampling the masses underfoot. The Revolution is dead; its spirit cries in the wilderness ... I have decided to leave Russia."

Truly was Trotsky able to boast that "at last the Soviet Government, with an iron broom, has rid Russia of anarchism". The Communists had forced

Alexander Berkman out of Russia. He and Emma were given their passports to attend the Anarchist Congress of 1921-22 in Germany.

★   ★   ★

The German government, however, refused them admission. But the Swedish authorities allowed them entry for a period of three months. Berkman then entered Germany illegally, and remained there for a year or two, while he wrote his pamphlets on Russia and the Kronstadt rebellion. After that he went to France. During this period, he helped organise committees to aid anarchists and libertarian socialists imprisoned in Russia. Unlike Emma Goldman he was not allowed to return to the United States. He settled in Paris. In 1925, his *The Bolshevik Myth (Diary 1920-1922)* was published in New York. Berkman also became involved in a controversy with Peter Arshinov and Nester Makhno regarding anarchist organisation. Arshinov had, like Berkman, Goldman, Makhno and others gone abroad; and on reaching Berlin in 1922, had founded the Group of Russian Anarchist-Communists Abroad, which three years later moved to Paris. Arshinov largely attributed the downfall of Russian anarchism to its perpetual state of disarray, which resulted in its inability to stand up to the better-organised Communists. Its only hope for revival, he said in 1926 when he set up his 'Organisation Platform', lay in the formation of a General Union of Anarchists with a strong central committee to co-ordinate action and policy. He was supported by Makhno. But Alexander Berkman, together with Emma Goldman, Volin and others, opposed them. Berkman accused them of advocating an Anarchist-Communist Party. "The trouble with most of our people," he said, "is that they will not see that Bolshevik methods cannot lead to liberty, that methods and issues are in essence and effects identical."

It was about this time that both Alexander Berkman and Emma Goldman has second thoughts about terrorism and violence. "I am in general now not in favour of terroristic tactics, except in very exceptional circumstances," he wrote to Emma in November 1928. She replied that "acts of violence except as demonstrations of a sensitive human soul have proved utterly useless ... I feel that violence in whatever form never has, and probably never will, bring constructive results". Neither she nor Berkman, however, became absolute pacifists. In *ABC of Anarchism* Berkman devotes a whole chapter ('Is Anarchism Violence?') to the subject violence. He returns to it in the last chapter, 'Defence of the Revolution'. In 1929, when he was working on that chapter, he wrote to Emma: "There are moments when I feel that the revolution cannot work on anarchist principles. But once the old methods are followed, they never lead to anarchism." Berkman was now just on 60, and was already a sick man. In a fit of depression, he wrote to Pierre Ramus in August 1935: "The old guard is passing away and there are almost none of the younger generation to take its place, or at least to do the work that must be done if the world is ever to see a better day." At the beginning of 1936 he underwent a serious prostate operation and in March he had a second. Both were unsuccessful. He was left with the prospect of slowly dying in great pain. On 28th June 1936, he took his revolver and shot himself. He died just three weeks before Durruti and the Spanish anarchists took up the challenge against Franco and the Fascist reaction. Had he lived a little longer he may not have been quite so despondent about the younger generation. There will always be a new generation to take the place of the old. Of Alexander Berkman, Emma Goldman wrote:

"If only he had lived a little longer! But the many years in exile, the unbelievable humiliations to which he was subjected, having to beg the right to breathe from creepy officials, the enervating and exhausting struggle for existence, and his severe illness combined to make life intolerable. Alexander hated dependence; he hated to become a burden to those he loved, and so he did what he had always said he would do: he hastened his end by his own hand."

Peter E. Newell
December 1970

AUTHOR'S FOREWORD

I consider anarchism the most rational and practical conception of a
social life in freedom and harmony. I am convinced that its realisation
is a certainty in the course of human development.

The time of that realisation will depend on two factors: first, on how soon
existing conditions will grow physically and spiritually unbearable to
considerable portions of mankind, particularly to the labouring classes;
and, secondly, on the degree in which anarchist views will become
understood and accepted.

Our social institutions are founded on certain ideas; as long as the latter
are generally believed, the institutions built on them are safe. Government
remains strong because people think political authority and legal
compulsion necessary. Capitalism will continue as long as such an
economic system is considered adequate and just. The weakening of the
ideas which support the evil and oppressive present day conditions means
the ultimate breakdown of government and capitalism. Progress consists in
abolishing what man has outlived and substituting in its place a more
suitable environment.

It must be evident even to the casual observer that society is undergoing
a radical change in its fundamental conceptions. The World War and the
Russian Revolution are the main causes of it. The war has unmasked the
vicious character of capitalist competition and the murderous incompetency

of governments to settle quarrels among nations, or rather among the ruling financial cliques. It is because the people are losing faith in the old methods that the Great Powers are now compelled to discuss limitation of armaments and even the outlawing of war. It is not so long ago that the very suggestion of such a possibility met with the utmost scorn and ridicule.

Similarly the belief in other established institutions is breaking down. Capitalism still 'works', but doubt about its expediency and justice is gnawing at the heart of ever-widening social circles. The Russian Revolution has broadcast ideas and feelings that are undermining capitalist society, particularly its economic bases and the sanctity of private ownership of the means of social existence. For not only in Russia did the October change take place; it has influenced the masses throughout the world. The cherished superstition that what exists is permanent has been shaken beyond recovery.

The war, the Russian Revolution, and the post-war developments have combined also to disillusion vast numbers about socialism. It is literally true that, like Christianity, socialism has conquered the world by defeating itself. The socialist parties now run or help to run most of the European governments, but the people do not believe any more that they are different from other bourgeois regimes. They feel that socialism has failed and is bankrupt.

In like manner have the Bolsheviks proven that Marxian dogma and Leninist principles can lead only to dictatorship and reaction.

To the anarchist there is nothing surprising in all this. They have always claimed that the State is destructive to individual liberty and social harmony, and that only the abolition of coercive authority and material inequality can solve our political, economic, and national problems. But their arguments, though based on the age-long experience of man, seemed mere theory to the present generation, until the events of the last two decades have demonstrated in actual life the truth of the anarchist position.

The breakdown of socialism and Bolshevism has cleared the way for anarchism.

There is considerable literature on anarchism, but most of its larger works were written before the World War. The experience of the recent past has been vital and has made certain revisions necessary in the anarchist attitude and argumentation. Though the basic propositions remain the same, some modifications of practical application are dictated by the facts of current history. The lessons of the Russian Revolution in particular call for a new approach to various important problems, chief among them the character and activities of the social revolution.

Furthermore, anarchist books, with few exceptions, are not accessible to the understanding of the average reader. It is the common failing of most works dealing with social questions that they are written on the assumption that the reader is already familiar to a considerable extent with the subject, which is generally not the case at all. As a result there are very few books treating of social problems in a sufficiently simple and intelligible manner.

For the above reason I consider a re-statement of the anarchist position very much needed at this time – a re-statement in the plainest and clearest terms which can be understood by everyone. That is, an ABC of Anarchism.

With that object in view the following pages have been written.

Paris, 1928

A young Alexander Berkman in 1892

Chapter 1

INTRODUCTION

I want to tell you about anarchism.

I want to tell you what anarchism is, because I think it is well you should know it. Also because so little is known about it, and what is known is generally hearsay and mostly false.

I want to tell you about it, because I believe that anarchism is the finest and biggest thing man has ever thought of; the only thing that can give you liberty and well-being, and bring peace and joy to the world.

I want to tell you about it in such plain and simple language that there will be no misunderstanding it. Big words and high sounding phrases serve only to confuse. Straight thinking means plain speaking.

But before I tell you what anarchism is, I want to tell you what it is not.

That is necessary because so much falsehood has been spread about anarchism. Even intelligent persons often have entirely wrong notions about it. Some people talk about anarchism without knowing a thing about it. And some lie about anarchism, because they don't want you to know the truth about it.

Anarchism has many enemies; they won't tell you the truth about it. Why anarchism has enemies and who they are, you will see later, in the course of this story. Just now I can tell you that neither your political boss nor your employer, neither the capitalist nor the policeman will speak to you honestly about anarchism. Most of them know nothing about it, and all of them hate it. Their newspapers and publications – the capitalistic press – are also against it.

Even most socialists and Bolsheviks misrepresent anarchism. True, the majority of them don't know any better. But those who do know better also often lie about anarchism and speak of it as 'disorder and chaos'. You can see for yourself how dishonest they are in this: the greatest teachers of socialism – Karl Marx and Friedrich Engels – had taught that anarchism would come from socialism. They said that we must first have socialism, but that after socialism there will be anarchism, and that it would be a freer and more beautiful condition of society to live in than socialism. Yet the socialists, who swear by Marx and Engels, insist on calling anarchism 'chaos and disorder', which shows you how ignorant or dishonest they are.

The Bolsheviks do the same, although their greatest teacher, Lenin, had said that anarchism would follow Bolshevism, and that then it will be better and freer to live.

Therefore I must tell you, first of all, what anarchism is not.

It is *not* bombs, disorder, or chaos.

It is *not* robbery and murder.

It is *not* a war of each against all.

It is *not* a return to barbarism or to the wild state of man.

Anarchism is the very opposite of all that.

Anarchism means that you should be free; that no one should enslave you, boss you, rob you, or impose upon you.

It means that you should be free to do the things you want to do; and that you should not be compelled to do what you don't want to do.

It means that you should have a chance to choose the kind of a life you want to live, and live it without anybody interfering.

It means that the next fellow should have the same freedom as you, that every one should have the same rights and liberties.

It means that all men are brothers, and that they should live like brothers, in peace and harmony.

That is to say, that there should be no war, no violence used by one set of men against another, no monopoly and no poverty, no oppression, no taking advantage of your fellow-man.

In short, anarchism means a condition or society where all men and women are free, and where all enjoy equally the benefits of an ordered and sensible life.

"Can that be?" you ask; "and how?"

"Not before we all become angels," your friend remarks.

Well, let us talk it over. Maybe I can show you that we can be decent and live as decent folks even without growing wings.

Chapter 2

IS ANARCHISM VIOLENCE?

You have heard that anarchists throw bombs, that they believe in violence, and that anarchy means disorder and chaos. It is not surprising that you should think so. The press, the pulpit, and every one in authority constantly din it into your ears. But most of them know better, even if they have a reason for not telling you the truth. It is time you should bear it.

I mean to speak to you honestly and frankly, and you can take my word for it, because it happens that I am just one of those anarchists who are pointed out as men of violence and destruction. I ought to know, and I have nothing to hide.

"Now, does anarchism really mean disorder and violence?" you wonder.

No, my friend, it is capitalism and government which stand for disorder and violence. Anarchism is the very reverse of it; it means order without government and peace without violence.

"But is that possible?" you ask.

That is just what we are going to talk over now. But first your friend demands to know whether anarchists have never thrown bombs or ever used any violence.

Yes, anarchists have thrown bombs and have sometimes resorted to violence.

"There you are!" your friend exclaims. "I thought so."

But do not let us be hasty. If anarchists have sometimes employed violence, does it necessarily mean that anarchism means violence?

Ask yourself this question and try to answer it honestly.

When a citizen puts on a soldier's uniform, he may have to throw bombs and use violence. Will you say, then, that citizenship stands for bombs and violence?

You will indignantly resent the imputation. It simply means, you will reply, that *under certain conditions* a man may have to resort to violence. The man may happen to be a democrat, a monarchist, a socialist, Bolshevik, or anarchist.

You will find that this applies to all men and to all times.

Brutus killed Caesar because he feared his friend meant to betray the republic and become king. Not that Brutus "loved Caesar less but that he loved Rome more." Brutus was not an anarchist. He was a loyal republican.

William Tell, as folklore tells us, shot to death the tyrant in order to rid his country of oppression. Tell had never heard of anarchism.

I mention these instances to illustrate the fact that from time immemorial despots met their fate at the hands of outraged lovers of liberty. Such men were rebels against tyranny. They were generally patriots, democrats or republicans, occasionally socialists or anarchists. Their acts were cases of individual rebellion against wrong and injustice. Anarchism had nothing to do with it.

There was a time in ancient Greece when killing a despot was considered the highest virtue. Modern law condemns such acts, but human feeling seems to have remained the same in this matter as in the old days. The conscience of the world does not feel outraged by tyrannicide. Even if publicly not approved, the heart of mankind condones and often even secretly rejoices at such acts. Were there not thousands of patriotic youths in America willing to assassinate the German Kaiser whom they held responsible for starting the World War? Did not a French court recently acquit the man who killed Petlura to avenge the thousands of men, women and children murdered in the Petlura pogroms against the Jews of South Russia?

In every land, in all ages, there have been tyrannicides; that is, men and women who loved their country well enough to sacrifice even their own lives for it. Usually they were persons of no political party or idea, but simply haters of tyranny. Occasionally they were religious fanatics, like the devout Catholic Kullmann, who tried to assassinate Bismarck,* or the misguided enthusiast Charlotte Corday who killed Marat during the French Revolution.

In the United States three Presidents were killed by individual acts. Lincoln was shot in 1865, by John Wilkes Booth, who was a Southern Democrat; Garfield, in 1881, by Charles Jules Guiteau, a Republican; and McKinley, in 1901, by Leon Czolgosz. Out of the three only one was an anarchist.

The country that has the worst oppressors produces also the greatest number of tyrannicides, which is natural. Take Russia, for instance. With complete suppression of speech and press under the Tsars, there was no way of mitigating the despotic régime than by "putting the fear of God" into the tyrant's heart.

Those avengers were mostly sons and daughters of the highest nobility, idealistic youths who loved liberty and the people. With all other avenues closed, they felt themselves compelled to resort to the pistol and dynamite in the hope of alleviating the miserable conditions of their country. They were known as nihilists and terrorists. They were not anarchists.

In modem times individual acts of political violence have been even more frequent than in the past. The women suffragettes in England, for example, frequently resorted to it to propagate and carry out their demands for equal rights. In Germany, since the war, men of the most conservative political views have used such methods in the hope of re-establishing the kingdom. It was a monarchist who killed Karl Erzberger, the Prussian Minister of Finance; and Walter Rathenau, Minister of Foreign Affairs, was also laid low by a man of the same political party.

Why, the original cause of, or at least excuse for, the Great War itself was the killing of the Austrian heir to the throne by a Serbian patriot who had

---

* On 13th July 1874.

never heard of anarchism. In Germany, Hungary, France, Italy, Spain, Portugal, and in every other European country men of the most varied political views have resorted to acts of violence, not to speak of the wholesale political terror, practiced by organised bodies such as the Fascists in Italy, the Ku Klux Klan in America, or the Catholic Church in Mexico.

You see, then, that anarchists have no monopoly of political violence. The number of such acts by anarchists is infinitesimal as compared with those committed by persons of other political persuasions.

The truth is that in every country, in every social movement, violence has been a part of the struggle from time immemorial. Even the Nazarene, who came to preach the gospel of peace, resorted to violence to drive the money changers out of the temple.

As I have said, anarchists have no monopoly on violence. On the contrary, the teachings of anarchism are those of peace and harmony, of non-invasion, of the sacredness of life and liberty. But anarchists are human, like the rest of mankind, and perhaps more so. They are more sensitive to wrong and injustice, quicker to resent oppression, and therefore not exempt from occasionally voicing their protest by an act of violence. But such acts are an expression of individual temperament, not of any particular theory.

You might ask whether the holding of revolutionary ideas would not naturally influence a person toward deeds of violence. I do not think so, because we have seen that violent methods are also employed by people of the most conservative opinions. If persons of directly opposite political views commit similar acts, it is hardly reasonable to say that their ideas are responsible for such acts.

Like results have a like cause, but that cause is not to be found in political convictions; rather in individual temperament and the general feeling about violence.

"You may be right about temperament," you say. "I can see that revolutionary ideas are not the cause of political acts of violence, else every revolutionist would be committing such acts. But do not such views to some extent justify those who commit such acts?"

It may seem so at first sight. But if you think it over you will find that it is an entirely wrong idea. The best proof of it is that anarchists who hold exactly the same views about government and the necessity of abolishing it, often disagree entirely on the question of violence. Thus Tolstoyan anarchists and most Individualist anarchists condemn political violence, while other anarchists approve of or at least justify it.

Is it reasonable, then, to say that anarchist views are responsible for violence or in any way influence such acts?

Moreover, many anarchists who at one time believed in violence as a means of propaganda have changed their opinion about it and do not favour such methods any more. There was a time, for instance, when anarchists advocated individual acts of violence, known as "propaganda by deed." They did not expect to change government and capitalism into anarchism by such acts, nor did they think that the taking off of a despot would abolish despotism. No, terrorism was considered a means of avenging a popular wrong, inspiring fear in the enemy, and also calling attention to the evil against which the act of terror was directed. But most anarchists today do not believe any more in "propaganda by deed" and do not favour acts of that nature.

Experience has taught them that though such methods may have been justified and useful in the past, modern conditions of life make them unnecessary and even harmful to the spread of their ideas. But their ideas remain the same, which means that it was not anarchism which shaped their attitude to violence. It proves that it is not certain ideas or "isms" that lead to violence, but that some other causes bring it about.

We must therefore look somewhere else to find the right explanation.

As we have seen, acts of political violence have been committed not only by anarchists, socialists, and revolutionists of all kinds, but also by patriots and nationalists, by Democrats and Republicans, by suffragettes, by conservatives and reactionaries, by monarchists and royalists, and even by religionists and devout Christians.

We know now that it could not have been any particular idea or "ism" that influenced their acts, because the most varied ideas and "isms" produced similar deeds. I have given as the reason individual temperament and the general feeling about violence.

Here is the crux of the matter. What is this general feeling about violence? If we can answer this question correctly, the whole matter will be clear to us.

If we speak honestly, we must admit that every one believes in violence and practices it, however he may condemn it in others. In fact, all of the institutions we support and the entire life of present society are based on violence.

What is the thing we call government? Is it anything else but organised violence? The law orders you to do this or not to do that, and if you fail to obey, it will compel you by force. We are not discussing just now whether it is right or wrong, whether it should or should not be so. Just now we are interested in the fact that it is so – that all government, all law and authority finally rest on force and violence, on punishment or the fear of punishment.

Why, even spiritual authority, the authority of the church and of God rests on force and violence, because it is the fear of divine wrath and vengeance that wields power over you, compels you to obey, and even to believe against your own reason.

Wherever you turn you will find that our entire life is built on violence or the fear of it. From earliest childhood you are subjected to the violence of parents or elders. At home, in school, in the office, factory, field, or shop, it is always someone's *authority* which keeps you obedient and compels you to do his will.

The right to compel you is called authority. Fear of punishment has been made into duty and is called obedience.

In this atmosphere of force and violence, of authority and obedience, of duty, fear and punishment we all grow up; we breathe it throughout our lives. We are so steeped in the spirit of violence that we never stop to ask whether violence is right or wrong. We only ask if it is legal, whether the law permits it.

You don't question the right of the government to kill, to confiscate and imprison. If a private person should be guilty of the things the government is doing all the time, you'd brand him a murderer, thief, and scoundrel. But as long as the violence committed is "lawful" you approve of it and submit to it. So it is not really violence that you object to, but to people using violence "unlawfully".

This lawful violence and the fear of it dominate our whole existence, individual and collective. Authority controls our lives from the cradle to the grave – authority parental, priestly and divine, political, economic, social, and moral. But whatever the character of that authority, it is always the same executioner wielding power over you through your fear of punishment in one form or another. You are afraid of God and the devil, of the priest and the neighbour, of your employer and boss, of the politician and policeman, of the judge and the jailer, of the law and the government. All your life is a long chain of fears – fears which bruise your body and lacerate your soul. On those fears is based the authority of God, of the church, of parents, of capitalist and ruler.

Look into your heart and see if what I say is not true. Why, even among children the ten-year-old Johnny bosses his younger brother or sister by the authority of his greater physical strength, just as Johnny's father bosses him by his superior strength, and by Johnny's dependence on his support. You stand for the authority of priest and preacher because you think they can "call down the wrath of God upon your head". You submit to the domination of boss, judge, and government because of their power to deprive you of work, to ruin your business, to put you in prison – a power, by the way, that you yourself have given into their hands.

So authority rules your whole life, the authority of the past and the present, of the dead and the living, and your existence is a continuous invasion and violation of yourself, a constant subjection to the thoughts and the will of someone else.

And as you are invaded and violated, so you subconsciously revenge yourself by invading and violating others over whom you have authority or can exercise compulsion, physical or moral. In this way all life has become a crazy quilt of authority, of domination and submission, of command and obedience, of coercion and subjection, of rulers and ruled, of violence and force in a thousand and one forms.

Can you wonder that even idealists are still held in the meshes of this spirit of authority and violence, and are often impelled by their feelings and environment to invasive acts entirely at variance with their ideas?

We are all still barbarians who resort to force and violence to settle our doubts, difficulties, and troubles. Violence is the method of ignorance, the weapon of the weak. The strong of heart and brain need no violence, for they are irresistible in their consciousness of being right. The further we get away from primitive man and the hatchet age, the less recourse we shall have to force and violence. The more enlightened man will become, the less he will employ compulsion and coercion. The really civilised man will divest himself of all fear and authority. He will rise from the dust and stand erect: he will bow to no tsar either in heaven or on earth. He will become fully human when he will scorn to rule and refuse to be ruled. He will be truly free only when there shall be no more masters.

Anarchism is the ideal of such a condition; of a society without force and compulsion, where all men shall be equals, and live in freedom, peace, and harmony.

The word anarchy comes from the Greek, meaning without force, without violence or government, because government is the very fountainhead of violence, constraint, and coercion.

Anarchy* therefore does not mean disorder and chaos, as you thought before. On the contrary, it is the very reverse of it; it means no government, which is freedom and liberty. Disorder is the child of authority and compulsion. Liberty is the mother of order.

"A beautiful ideal," you say; "but only angels are fit for it."

Let us see, then, if we can grow the wings we need for that ideal state of society.

---

* Anarchy refers to the condition. Anarchism is the theory or teaching about it.

Chapter 3

WHAT IS ANARCHISM?

"Can you tell us briefly," your friend asks, "what anarchism really is?"

I shall try. In the fewest words, anarchism teaches that we can live in a society where there is no compulsion of any kind.

A life without compulsion naturally means liberty; it means freedom from being forced or coerced, a chance to lead the life that suits you best.

You cannot lead such a life unless you do away with the institutions that curtail your liberty and interfere with your life, the conditions that compel you to act differently from the way you really would like to.

What are those institutions and conditions? Let us see what we have to do away with in order to secure a free and harmonious life. Once we know what has to be abolished and what must take its place, we shall also find the way to do it.

What must be abolished, then, to secure liberty?

First of all, of course, the thing that invades you most, that handicaps or prevents your free activity; the thing that interferes with your liberty and compels you to live differently from what would be your own choice.

That thing is government.

Take a good look at it and you will see that government is the greatest invader; more than that, the worst criminal man has ever known of. It fills the world with violence, with fraud and deceit, with oppression and misery.

As a great thinker once said, "its breath is poison." It corrupts everything it touches.

"Yes, government means violence and it is evil," you admit; "but can we do without it?"

That is just what we want to talk over. Now, if I should ask you whether you need government, I'm sure you would answer that you don't, but that it is for the others that it is needed.

But if you should ask any one of those "others," he would reply as you do: he would say that he does not need it, but that it is necessary "for the others."

Why does every one think that he can be decent enough without the policeman, but that the club is needed for "the others"?

"People would rob and murder each other if there were no government and no law," you say.

If they really would, why would they? Would they do it just for the pleasure of it or because of certain reasons? Maybe if we examine their reasons, we'd discover the cure for them.

Suppose you and I and a score of others had suffered shipwreck and found ourselves on an island rich with fruit of every kind. Of course, we'd get to work to gather the food. But suppose one of our number should declare that it all belongs to him, and that no one shall have a single morsel unless he first pays him tribute for it. We would be indignant, wouldn't we? We'd laugh at his pretensions. If he'd try to make trouble about it, we might throw him into the sea, and it would serve him right, would it not?

Suppose further that we ourselves and our forefathers had cultivated the island and stocked it with everything needed for life and comfort, and that someone should arrive and claim it all as his. What would we say? We'd ignore him, wouldn't we? We might tell him that he could share with us and join us in our work. But suppose that he insists on his ownership and that he produces a slip of paper and says that it proves that everything belongs to him? We'd tell him he's crazy and we'd go about our business. But if he should have a government back of him, he would appeal to it for the protection of 'his rights', and the government would send police and soldiers who would evict us and put the 'lawful owner in possession'.

That is the function of government; that is what government exists for and what it is doing all the time.

Now, do you still think that without this thing called government we should rob and murder each other?

Is it not rather true that *with* government we rob and murder? Because government does not secure us in our rightful possessions, but on the contrary takes them away for the benefit of those who have no right to them, as we have seen in previous chapters.*

If you should wake up tomorrow morning and learn that there is no government any more, would your first thought be to rush out into the street and kill someone? No, you know that is nonsense. We speak of sane, normal men. The insane man who wants to kill does not first ask whether there is or isn't any government. Such men belong to the care of physicians and alienists; they should be placed in hospitals to be treated for their malady.

The chances are that if you or Johnson should awaken to find that there is no government, you would get busy arranging your life under the new conditions.

It is very likely, of course, that if you should then see people gorge themselves while you go hungry, you would demand a chance to eat, and you would be perfectly right in that. And so would every one else, which means that people would not stand for any one hogging all the good things of life: they would want to share in them. It means further that the poor would refuse to stay poor while others wallow in luxury. It means that the worker will decline to give up his product to the boss who claims to 'own' the factory and everything that is made there. It means that the farmer will not permit thousands of acres to lie idle while he has not enough soil to support himself and family. It means that no one will be permitted to monopolise the land or the machinery of production. It means that private ownership of the *sources of life* will not be tolerated any more. It will be considered the greatest crime for some to own more than they can use in a

---

* i.e. in Part 1 of Berkman's original book, see Publisher's Note.

dozen lifetimes, while their neighbours have not enough bread for their children. It means that all men will share in the social wealth, and that all will help to produce that wealth.

It means, in short, that for the first time in history right, justice and equality would triumph instead of law.

You see therefore that doing away with government also signifies the abolition of monopoly and of personal ownership of the means of production and distribution.

It follows that when government is abolished, wage slavery and capitalism must also go with it, because they cannot exist without the support and protection of government. Just as the man who would claim a monopoly of the island, of which I spoke before, could not put through his crazy claim without the help of government.

Such a condition of things where there would be liberty instead of government would be *Anarchy*. And where equality of use would take the place of private ownership, would be *Communism*.

It would be *Communist Anarchism*.

"Oh, communism," your friend exclaims, "but you said you were not a Bolshevik!"

No, I am not a Bolshevik, because the Bolsheviks want a powerful government or state, while anarchism means doing away with the state or government altogether.

"But are not the Bolsheviki communists?" you demand.

Yes, the Bolsheviki are communists, but they want their dictatorship, their government, to compel people to live in communism. Anarchist communism, on the contrary, means voluntary communism, communism from free choice.

"I see the difference. It would be fine, of course;" your friend admits. "But do you really think it possible?"

Chapter 4

IS ANARCHY POSSIBLE?

"It might be possible," you say, "if we could do without government. But can we?"

Perhaps we can best answer your question by examining your own life.

What role does the government play in your existence? Does it help you live? Does it feed, clothe, and shelter you? Do you need it to help you work or play? If you are ill, do you call the physician or the policeman? Can the government give you greater ability than nature endowed you with? Can it save you from sickness, old age, or death?

Consider your daily life and you will find that in reality the government is no factor in it at all except when it begins to interfere in your affairs, when it compels you to do certain things or prohibits you from doing others. It forces you, for instance, to pay taxes and support it, whether you want to or not. It makes you don a uniform and join the army. It invades your personal life, orders you about, coerces you, prescribes your behaviour, and generally treats you as it pleases. It tells you even what you must believe and punishes you for thinking and acting otherwise. It directs you what to eat and drink, and imprisons or shoots you for disobeying. It commands you and dominates every step of your life. It treats you as a bad boy or as an *irresponsible* child who needs the strong hand of a guardian, but if you disobey it holds you *responsible*, nevertheless.

We shall consider later the details of life under anarchy and see what conditions and institutions will exist in that form of society, how they will function, and what effect they are likely to have upon man.

For the present we want to make sure first that such a condition is possible, that anarchy is practicable.

What is the existence of the average man today? Almost all your time is given to earning your livelihood. You are so busy making a living that you hardly have time left to live, to enjoy life. Neither the time nor the money. You are lucky if you have some source of support, some job. Now and then comes slack-time: there is unemployment and thousands are thrown out of work, every year, in every country.

That time means no income, no wages. It results in worry and privation, in disease, desperation, and suicide. It spells poverty and crime. To alleviate that poverty we build homes of charity, poorhouses, free hospitals, all of which you support with your taxes. To prevent crime and to punish the criminals it is again you who have to support police, detectives, state forces, judges, lawyers, prisons, keepers. Can you imagine anything more senseless and impractical? The legislatures pass laws, the judges interpret them, the various officials execute them, the police track and arrest the criminal, and finally the prison warden gets him into custody. Numerous persons and institutions are busy keeping the jobless man from stealing and punish him if he tries to. Then he is provided with the means of existence, the lack of which had made him break the law in the first place. After a shorter or longer term he is turned loose. If he fails to get work he begins the same round of theft, arrest, trial, and imprisonment all over again.

This is a rough but typical illustration of the stupid character of our system; stupid and inefficient. Law and government support that system.

Is it not peculiar that most people imagine we could not do without government, when in fact our real life has no connection with it whatever, no need of it, and is only interfered with where law and government seep in?

"But security and public order," you object, "could we have that without law and government? Who will protect us against the criminal?"

The truth is that what is called "law and order" is really the worst disorder, as we have seen in previous chapters.* What little order and peace we do have is due to the good common sense and joint efforts of the people, mostly in spite of the government. Do you need government to tell you not to step in front of a moving automobile? Do you need it to order you not to jump off the Brooklyn Bridge or from the Eiffel Tower?

Man is a social being: he cannot exist alone; he lives in communities or societies. Mutual need and common interests result in certain arrangements to afford us security and comfort. Such co-working is free, voluntary; it needs no compulsion by any government. You join a sporting club or a singing society because your inclinations lie that way, and you co-operate with the other members without any one coercing you. The man of science, the writer, the artist, and the inventor seek their own kind for inspiration and mutual work. Their impulses and needs are their best urge: the interference of any government or authority can only hinder their efforts.

All through life you will find that the needs and inclinations of people make for association, for mutual protection and help. That is the difference between managing things and governing men; between doing something from free choice and being compelled. It is the difference between liberty and constraint, between anarchism and government, because anarchism means voluntary cooperation instead of forced participation. It means harmony and order in place of interference and disorder.

"But who will protect us against crime and criminals?" you demand.

Rather ask yourself whether government really protects us against them. Does not government itself create and uphold conditions which make for crime? Does not the invasion and violence upon which all governments rest cultivate the spirit of intolerance and persecution, of hatred and more violence? Does not crime increase with the growth of poverty and injustice fostered by government? Is not government itself the greatest injustice and crime?

Crime is the result of economic conditions, of social inequality, of wrongs and evils of which government and monopoly are the parents. Government and law can only punish the criminal. They neither cure nor prevent crime.

---

* On 13th July 1874.

The only real cure for crime is to abolish its causes, and this the government can never do because it is there to preserve those very causes. Crime can be eliminated only by doing away with the conditions that create it. Government cannot do it.

Anarchism means to do away with those conditions. Crimes resulting from government, from its oppression and injustice, from inequality and poverty, will disappear under anarchy. These constitute by far the greatest percentage of crime.

Certain other crimes will persist for some time, such as those resulting from jealousy, passion, and from the spirit of coercion and violence which dominates the world today. But these, the offspring of authority and possession, will also gradually disappear under wholesome conditions with the passing away of the atmosphere that cultivated them.

Anarchy will therefore neither breed crime nor offer any soil for its thriving. Occasional anti-social acts will be looked upon as survivals of former diseased conditions and attitudes, and will be treated as an unhealthy state of mind rather than as crime.

Anarchy would begin by feeding the 'criminal' and securing him work instead of first watching him, arresting, trying, and imprisoning him, and finally ending by feeding him and the many others who have to watch and feed him. Surely even this example shows how much more sensible and simpler life would be under anarchism than now.

The truth is, present life is impractical, complex and confused, and not satisfactory from any point of view. That is why there is so much misery and discontent. The worker is not satisfied; nor is the master happy in his constant anxiety over 'bad times' involving loss of property and power. The spectre of fear for tomorrow dogs the steps of poor and rich alike.

Certainly the worker has nothing to lose by a change from government and capitalism to a condition of no government, of anarchy.

The middle classes are almost as uncertain of their existence as the workers. They are dependent upon the good will of the manufacturer and wholesaler, of the large combines of industry and capital, and they are always in danger of bankruptcy and ruin.

Even the big capitalist has little to lose by the changing of the present-day system to one of anarchy, for under the latter every one would be assured of living and comfort; the fear of competition would be eliminated with the abolition of private ownership. Every one would have full and unhindered opportunity to live and enjoy his life to the utmost of his capacity.

Add to this the consciousness of peace and harmony; the feeling that comes with freedom from financial or material worries; the realisation that you are in a friendly world with no envy or business rivalry to disturb your mind; in a world of brothers, in an atmosphere of liberty and general welfare.

It is almost impossible to conceive of the wonderful opportunities which would open up to man in a society of communist anarchism. The scientist could fully devote himself to his beloved pursuits, without being harassed about his daily bread. The inventor would find every facility at his disposal to benefit humanity by his discoveries and inventions. The writer, the poet, the artist – all would rise on the wings of liberty and social harmony to greater heights of attainment.

Only then would justice and right come into their own. Do not underestimate the role of these sentiments in the life of man or nation. We do not live by bread alone. True, existence is not possible without opportunity to satisfy our physical needs. But the gratification of these by no means constitutes all of life. Our present system of civilisation has, by disinheriting millions, made the belly the centre of the universe, so to speak. But in a sensible society, with plenty for all, the matter of mere existence, the security of a livelihood would be considered self-evident and free as the air is for all. The feelings of human sympathy, of justice and right would have a chance to develop, to be satisfied, to broaden and grow. Even today the sense of justice and fair play is still alive in the heart of man, in spite of centuries of repression and perversion. It has not been exterminated, it cannot be exterminated because it is inborn, innate in man, an instinct as strong as that of self-preservation, and just as vital to our happiness. For not all the misery we have in the world today comes from the lack of material welfare. Man can better stand starvation than the consciousness of injustice. The consciousness that you are treated unjustly will rouse you to protest and rebellion just as quickly as hunger, perhaps even quicker. Hunger may be the immediate cause of every rebellion or uprising, but beneath it is the slumbering antagonism and hatred of the masses against those at whose hands they are suffering injustice and wrong. The truth is that right and justice play a far more important role in our lives than most people are aware of. Those who would deny this know as little of human nature as of history. In everyday life you constantly see people grow indignant at what they consider to be an injustice. "That isn't right," is the instinctive protest of man when he feels wrong done. Of course, every one's conception of wrong and right depends on his traditions, environment and bringing up. But whatever his conception, his natural impulse is to resent what he thinks wrong and unjust.

Historically the same holds true. More rebellions and wars have been fought for ideas of right and wrong than because of material reasons. Marxists may object that our views of right and wrong are themselves formed by economic conditions, but that in no way alters the fact that the sense of justice and right has at all times inspired people to heroism and self-sacrifice on behalf of ideals.

The Christs and the Buddhas of all ages were not prompted by material considerations but by their devotion to justice and right. The pioneers in every human endeavour have suffered calumny, persecution, even death, not for motives of personal aggrandisement but because of their faith in the justice of their cause. The John Husses, the Luthers, Brunos, Savonarolas, Gallileos and numerous other religious and social idealists fought and died championing the cause of right as they saw it. Similarly in paths of science, philosophy, art, poetry, and education men from the time of Socrates to modern days have devoted their lives to the service of truth and justice. In the field of political and social advancement, beginning with Moses and Spartacus, the noblest of humanity have consecrated themselves to ideals of liberty and equality. Nor is this compelling power of idealism limited only to exceptional individuals. The masses have always been inspired by it. The

American War of Independence, for instance, began with popular resentment in the Colonies against the injustice of taxation without representation. The Crusades continued for two hundred years in an effort to secure the Holy Land for the Christians. This religious ideal inspired six millions of men, even armies of children, to face untold hardships, pestilence, and death in the name of right and justice. Even the late World War, capitalistic as it was in cause and result, was fought by millions of men in the fond belief that it was being waged for a just cause, for democracy and the termination of all wars.

So all through history, past and modern, the sense of right and justice has inspired man, individually and collectively, to deeds of self-sacrifice and devotion, and raised him far above the mean drabness of his everyday existence. It is tragic, of course, that this idealism expressed itself in acts of persecution, violence, and slaughter. It was the viciousness and self-seeking of king, priest, and master, ignorance and fanaticism which determined those forms. But the spirit that filled them was that of right and justice. All past experience proves that this spirit is ever alive and that it is a powerful and dominant factor in the whole scale of human life.

The conditions of our present-day existence weaken and vitiate this noblest trait of man, pervert its manifestation, and turn it into channels of intolerance, persecution, hatred, and strife. But once man is freed from the corrupting influences of material interests, lifted out of ignorance and class antagonism, his innate spirit of right and justice would find new forms of expression, forms that would tend toward greater brotherhood and good will, toward individual peace and social harmony.

Only under anarchy could this spirit come into its full development. Liberated from the degrading and brutalising struggle for our daily bread, all sharing in labour and well-being, the best qualities of man's heart and mind would have opportunity for growth and beneficial application. Man would indeed become the noble work of nature that he has till now visioned himself only in his dreams.

It is for these reasons that anarchy is the ideal not only of some particular element or class, but of all humanity, because it would benefit, in the largest sense, all of us. For anarchism is the formulation of a universal and perennial desire of mankind.

Every man and woman, therefore, should be vitally interested in helping to bring anarchy about. They would surely do so if they but understood the beauty and justice of such a new life. Every human being who is not devoid of feeling and common sense is inclined to anarchism. Every one who suffers from wrong and injustice, from the evil, corruption, and filth of our present-day life, is instinctively sympathetic to anarchy. Every one whose heart is not dead to kindness, compassion, and fellow-sympathy must be interested in furthering it. Every one who has to endure poverty and misery, tyranny and oppression should welcome the coming of anarchy. Every liberty and justice-loving man and woman should help realise it.

And foremost and most vitally of all the subjected and submerged of the world must be interested in it. Those who build palaces and live in hovels; who set the table of life but are not permitted to partake of the repast; who create the wealth of the world and are disinherited; who fill life with joy and sunshine, and themselves remain scorned in the depths of darkness; the Samson of life shorn of his strength by the hand of fear and ignorance; the helpless Giant of labour, the proletariat of brain and brawn, the industrial and agrarian masses – these should most gladly embrace anarchy.

It is to them that anarchism makes the strongest appeal; it is they who, first and foremost, must work for the new day that is to give them back their inheritance and bring liberty and well-being, joy and sunshine to the whole of mankind.

"A splendid thing," you remark; "but will it work? And how shall we attain it?"

Chapter 5

WILL COMMUNIST ANARCHISM
WORK?

As we have seen in the preceding chapter, no life can be free and secure, harmonious and satisfactory unless it is built on principles of justice and fair play. The first requirement of justice is equal liberty and opportunity.

Under government and exploitation there can be neither equal liberty nor equal opportunity – hence all the evils and troubles of present-day society.

Communist anarchism is based on the understanding of this incontrovertible truth. It is founded an the principle of non-invasiveness and non-coercion; in other words, on liberty and opportunity.

Life on such a basis fully satisfies the demands of justice. You are to be entirely free, and everybody else is to enjoy equal liberty, which means that no one has a right to compel or force another, for coercion of any kind is interference with your liberty.

Similarly equal opportunity is the heritage of all. Monopoly and the private ownership of the means of existence are therefore eliminated as an abridgement of the equal opportunity of all.

If we keep in mind this simple principle of equal liberty and opportunity, we shall be able to solve the questions involved in building a society of communist anarchism.

Politically, then, man will recognise no authority which can force or coerce him. Government will be abolished.

Economically he will permit no exclusive possession of the sources of life in order to preserve his opportunity of free access.

Monopoly of land, private ownership of the machinery of production, distribution, and communication can therefore not be tolerated under anarchy. Opportunity to use what every one needs in order to live must be free to all.

In a nutshell, then, the meaning of communist anarchism is this: the abolition of government, of coercive authority and all its agencies, and joint ownership – which means free and equal participation in the general work and welfare.

"You said that anarchy will secure economic equality," remarks your friend. "Does that mean equal pay for all?"

It does. Or, what amounts to the same, equal participation in the public welfare. Because, as we already know, labour is social. No man can create anything all by himself, by his own efforts. Now, then, if labour is social, it stands to reason that the results of it, the wealth produced, must also be social, belong to the collectivity. No person can therefore justly lay claim to the exclusive ownership of the social wealth. It is to be enjoyed by all alike.

"But why not give each according to the value of his work?" you ask.

Because there is no way by which value can be measured. That is the difference between value and price. Value is what a thing is worth, while price is what it can be sold or bought for in the market. What a thing is worth no one really can tell. Political economists generally claim that the value of a commodity is the amount of labour required to produce it, of "socially necessary labour," as Marx says. But evidently it is not a just standard of measurement. Suppose the carpenter worked three hours to make a kitchen chair, while the surgeon took only half an hour to perform an operation that saved your life. If the amount of labour used determines value, then the chair is worth more than your life. Obvious nonsense, of course. Even if you should count in the years of study and practice the surgeon needed to make him capable of performing the operation, how are you going to decide what 'an hour of operating' is worth? The carpenter and mason also had to be trained before they could do their work properly, but you don't figure in those years of apprenticeship when you contract for some work with them. Besides, there is also to be considered the particular ability and aptitude that every worker, writer, artist or physician must exercise in his labours. That is a purely individual, personal factor. How are you going to estimate its value?

That is why value cannot be determined. The same thing may be worth a lot to one person while it is worth nothing or very little to another. It may be worth much or little even to the same person, at different times. A diamond, a painting, or a book may be worth a great deal to one man and very little to another. A loaf of bread will be worth a great deal to you when you are hungry, and much less when you are not. Therefore the real value of a thing cannot be ascertained; it is an unknown quantity.

But the price is easily found out. If there are five loaves of bread to be had and ten persons want to get a loaf each, the price of bread will rise. If there are ten loaves and only five buyers, then it will fall. Price depends on supply and demand.

The exchange of commodities by means of prices leads to profit making, to taking advantage and exploitation; in short, to some form of capitalism. If you do away with profits, you cannot have any price system, nor any system of wages or payment. That means that exchange must be according to value. But as value is uncertain or not ascertainable, exchange must consequently be free, without "equal" value, since such does not exist. In other words, labour and its products must be exchanged without price, without profit, freely, according to necessity. This logically leads to ownership in common and to joint use. Which is a sensible, just, and equitable system, and is known as communism.

"But is it just that all should share alike?" you demand. "The man of brains and the dullard, the efficient and the inefficient, all the same? Should there be no distinction, no special recognition for those of ability?"

Let me in turn ask you, my friend, shall we punish the man whom nature has not endowed as generously as his stronger or more talented neighbour? Shall we add injustice to the handicap nature has put upon him? All we can reasonably expect from any man is that he do his best – can any one do more? And if John's best is not as good as his brother Jim's, it is his misfortune, but in no case a fault to be punished.

There is nothing more dangerous than discrimination. The moment you begin discriminating against the less capable, you establish conditions that breed dissatisfaction and resentment: you invite envy, discord, and strife. You would think it brutal to withhold from the less capable the air or water they need. Should not the same principle apply to the other wants of man? After all, the matter of food, clothing, and shelter is the smallest item in the world's economy.

The surest way to get one to do his best is not by discriminating against him, but by treating him on an equal footing with others. That is the most effective encouragement and stimulus. It is just and human.

"But what will you do with the lazy man, the man who does not want to work?" inquires your friend.

That is an interesting question, and you will probably be very much surprised when I say that there is really no such thing as laziness. What we call a lazy man is generally a square man in a round hole. That is, the right man in the wrong place. And you will always find that when a fellow is in the wrong place, he will be inefficient or shiftless. For so-called laziness and a good deal of inefficiency are merely unfitness, misplacement. If you are compelled to do the thing you are unfitted for by your inclinations or temperament, you will be inefficient at it; if you are forced to do work you are not interested in, you will be lazy at it.

Every one who has managed affairs in which large numbers of men were employed can substantiate this. Life in prison is a particularly convincing proof of the truth of it and, after all, present-day existence for most people is but that of a larger jail. Every prison warden will tell you that inmates put to tasks for which they have no ability or interest are always lazy and subject to continuous punishment. But as soon as these 'refractory convicts' are assigned to work that appeals to their leanings, they become 'model men', as the jailers term them.

Russia has also signally demonstrated the verity of it. It has shown how little we know of human potentialities and of the effect of environment upon them – how we mistake wrong conditions for bad conduct. Russian refugees, leading a miserable and insignificant life in foreign lands, on returning home and finding in the Revolution a proper field for their activities, have accomplished most wonderful work in their right sphere, have developed into brilliant organisers, builders of railroads and creators of industry. Among the Russian names best known abroad today are those of men considered shiftless and inefficient under conditions where their ability and energies could not find proper application.

That is human nature: efficiency in a certain direction means inclination and capability for it; industry and application signify interest. That is why there is so much inefficiency and laziness in the world today. For who indeed is nowadays in his right place? Who works at what he really likes and is interested in?

Under present conditions there is little choice given the average man to devote himself to the tasks that appeal to his leanings and preferences. The accident of your birth and social station generally predetermines your trade or profession. The son of the financier does not, as a rule, become a woodchopper, though he may be more fit to handle logs than bank accounts. The middle classes send their children to colleges which turn them into doctors, lawyers, or engineers. But if your parents were workers who could not afford to let you study, the chances are that you will take any job which is offered you, or enter some trade that happens to afford you an apprenticeship. Your particular situation will decide your work or profession, not your natural preferences, inclinations, or abilities. Is it any wonder, then, that most people, the overwhelming majority, in fact, are misplaced? Ask the first hundred men you meet whether they would have selected the work they are doing, or whether they would continue in it, if they were free to choose, and ninety-nine of them will admit that they would prefer some other occupation. Necessity and material advantages, or the hope of them, keep most people in the wrong place.

It stands to reason that a person can give the best of himself only when his interest is in his work, when he feels a natural attraction to it, when he likes it. Then he will be industrious and efficient. The things the craftsman produced in the days before modern capitalism were objects of joy and beauty, because the artisan loved his work. Can you expect the modern drudge in the ugly huge factory to make beautiful things? He is part of the machine, a cog in the soulless industry, his labour mechanical, forced. Add to this his feeling that he is not working for himself but for the benefit of someone else, and that he hates his job or at best has no interest in it except that it secures his weekly wage. The result is shirking, inefficiency, laziness.

The need of activity is one of the most fundamental urges of man. Watch the child and see how strong is his instinct for action, for movement, for doing something. Strong and continuous. It is the same with the healthy man. His energy and vitality demand expression. Permit him to do the work of his choice, the thing he loves, and his application will know neither weariness nor shirking. You can observe this in the factory worker when he is lucky enough to own a garden or a patch of ground to raise some flowers or vegetables on. Tired from his toil as he is, he enjoys the hardest labour for his own benefit, done from free choice.

Under anarchism each will have the opportunity of following whatever occupation will appeal to his natural inclinations and aptitude. Work will become a pleasure instead of the deadening drudgery it is today. Laziness will be unknown, and the things created by interest and love will be objects of beauty and joy.

"But can labour ever become a pleasure?" you demand.

Labour is toil today, unpleasant, exhausting, and wearisome. But usually it is not the work itself that is so hard: it is the conditions under which you are compelled to labour that make it so. Particularly the long hours, unsanitary workshops, bad treatment, insufficient pay, and so on. Yet the most unpleasant work could be made lighter by improving the environment. Take gutter cleaning, for instance. It is dirty work and poorly paid for. But suppose, for example, that you should get 20 dollars a day instead of 5 dollars for such work. You will immediately find your job much lighter and pleasanter. The number of applicants for the work would increase at once. Which means that men are not lazy, not afraid of hard and unpleasant labour if it is properly rewarded. But such work is considered menial and is looked down upon. Why is it considered menial? Is it not most useful and absolutely necessary? Would not epidemics sweep our city but for the street and gutter cleaners? Surely, the men who keep our town clean and sanitary are real benefactors, more vital to our health and welfare than the family physician. From the viewpoint of social usefulness the street cleaner is the professional colleague of the doctor: the latter treats us when we are ill, but the former helps us keep well. Yet the physician is looked up to and respected, while the street cleaner is slighted. Why? Is it because the street cleaner's work is dirty? But the surgeon often has much 'dirtier' jobs to perform. Then why is the street cleaner scorned? Because he *earns little*.

In our perverse civilisation things are valued according to money standards. Persons doing the most useful work are lowest in the social scale when their employment is ill paid. Should something happen, however, that would cause the street cleaner to get 100 dollars a day, while the physician earns, the 'dirty' street cleaner would immediately rise in estimation and social station, and from the 'filthy labourer' he would become the much-sought man of good income.

You see that it is pay, remuneration, *the wage scale*, not worth or merit, that today – under our system of profit – determines the value of work as well as the 'worth' of a man.

A sensible society – under anarchist conditions – would have entirely different standards of judging such matters. People will then be appreciated according to their *willingness to be socially useful.*

Can you perceive what great changes such a new attitude would produce? Every one yearns for the respect and admiration of his fellow men; it is a tonic we cannot live without. Even in prison I have seen how the clever pickpocket or safe blower longs for the appreciation of his friends and how hard he tries to earn their good estimate of him. The opinions of our circle rule our behaviour. The social atmosphere to a profound degree determines our values and our attitude. Your personal experience will tell you how true this is, and therefore you will not be surprised when I say that in an anarchist society it will be the most useful and difficult toil that men will seek rather than the lighter job. If you consider this, you will have no more fear of laziness or shirking.

But the hardest and most onerous task could be made easier and cleaner than is the case today. The capitalist employer does not care to spend money, if he can help it, to make the toil of his employees pleasanter and brighter. He will introduce improvements only when he hopes to gain larger profits thereby, but he will not go to extra expense out of purely humanitarian reasons. Though here I must remind you that the more intelligent employers are beginning to see that it pays to improve their factories, make them more sanitary and hygienic, and generally better the conditions of labour. They realise it is a good investment: it results in the increased contentment and consequent greater efficiency of their workers. The principle is sound. Today, of course, it is being exploited for the sole purpose of bigger profits. But under anarchism it would be applied not for the sake of personal gain, but in the interest of the workers' health, for the lightening of labour. Our progress in mechanics is so great and continually advancing that most of the hard toil could be eliminated by the use of modern machinery and labour saving devices. In many industries, as in coal mining, for instance, new safety and sanitary appliances are not introduced because of the masters' indifference to the welfare of their employees and on account of the expenditure involved. But in a non-profit system technical science would work exclusively with the aim of making labour safer, healthier, lighter, and more pleasant.

"But however light you'll make work, eight hours a day of it is no pleasure," objects your friend.

You are perfectly right. But did you ever stop to consider why we have to work eight hours a day? Do you know that not so long ago people used to slave twelve and fourteen hours, and that it is still the case in backward countries like China and India?

It can be statistically proven that three hours' work a day, at most, is sufficient to feed, shelter, and clothe the world and supply it not only with necessities but also with all modern comforts of life. The point is that not one man in five is today doing any productive work. The entire world is supported by a small minority of toilers.

First of all, consider the amount of work done in present-day society that would become unnecessary under anarchist conditions. Take the armies and navies of the world, and think how many millions of men would be released for useful and productive effort once war is abolished, as would of course be the case under anarchy.

In every country today labour supports the millions who contribute nothing to the welfare of the country, who create nothing, and perform no useful work whatever. Those millions are only consumers, without being producers. In the United States, for instance, out of a population of 120 millions there are less than 30 million workers, farmers included. A similar situation is the rule in every land.

Is it any wonder that labour has to toil long hours, since there are only 30 workers to every 120 persons? The large business classes with their clerks, assistants, agents, and commercial travellers; the courts with their judges, record keepers, bailiffs, etc.; the legion of attorneys with their staffs; the militia and police forces; the churches and monasteries; the charity institutions and poorhouses; the prisons with their wardens, officers, keepers, and the non-productive convict population; the army of advertisers and their helpers, whose business it is to persuade you to buy what you don't want or need, not to speak of the numerous elements that live luxuriously in entire idleness. All these mount into the millions in every country.

Now, if all those millions would apply themselves to useful labour, would the worker have to drudge eight hours a day? If 30 men have to put in eight hours to perform a certain task, how much less time would it take 120 men to accomplish the same thing? I don't want to burden you with statistics, but there are enough data to prove that less than 3 hours of daily physical effort would be sufficient to do the world's work.

Can you doubt that even the hardest toil would become a pleasure instead of the cursed slavery it is at present, if only three hours a day were required, and that under the most sanitary and hygienic conditions, in an atmosphere of brotherhood and respect for labour?

But it is not difficult to foresee the day when even those short hours would be still further reduced. For we are constantly improving our technical methods, and new labour saving machinery is being invented all the time. Mechanical progress means less work and greater comforts, as you can see by comparing life in the United States with that in China or India. In the latter countries they toil long hours to secure the barest necessities of existence, while in America even the average labourer enjoys a much higher standard of living with fewer hours of work. The advance of science and invention signifies more leisure for the pursuits we love.

I have sketched in large, broad outline the possibilities under a sensible system where profit is abolished. It is not necessary to go into the minute details of such a social condition: sufficient has been said to show that communist anarchism means the greatest material welfare with a life of liberty for each and all.

We can visualise the time when labour will have become a pleasant exercise, a joyous application of physical effort to the needs of the world. Man will then look back at our present day and wonder that work could ever have been slavery, and question the sanity of a generation that suffered less than one fifth of its population to earn the bread for the rest by the sweat of their brow while those others idled and wasted their time, their health, and the people's wealth. They will wonder that the freest satisfaction of man's needs could have ever been considered as anything but self-evident, or that people naturally seeking the same objects insisted on making life hard and miserable by mutual strife. They will refuse to believe that the whole existence of man was a continuous struggle for food in a world rich with luxuries, a struggle that left the great majority neither time nor strength for the higher quest of the heart and mind.

"But will not life under anarchy, in economic and social equality mean general leveling?" you ask.

No, my friend, quite the contrary. Because equality does not mean an equal amount but equal *opportunity*. It does not mean, for instance, that if Smith needs five meals a day, Johnson also must have as many. If Johnson wants only three meals while Smith requires five, the quantity each consumes may be unequal, but both men are perfectly equal in the opportunity each has to consume as much as he needs, as much as his particular nature demands.

Do not make the mistake of identifying equality in liberty with the forced equality of the convict camp. True anarchist equality implies freedom, not quantity. It does not mean that every one must eat, drink, or wear the same things, do the same work, or live in the same manner. Far from it; the very reverse, in fact.

Individual needs and tastes differ, as appetites differ. It is *equal opportunity* to satisfy them that constitutes true equality.

Far from leveling, such equality opens the door for the greatest possible variety of activity and development. For human character is diverse, and only the repression of this diversity results in leveling, in uniformity and sameness. Free opportunity of expressing and acting out your individuality means development of natural dissimilarities and variations.

It is said that no two blades of grass are alike. Much less so are human beings. In the whole wide world no two persons are exactly similar even in physical appearance; still more dissimilar are they in their physiological, mental, and psychical make-up. Yet in spite of this diversity and of a thousand and one differentiations of character we compel people to be alike today. Our life and habits, our behaviour and manners, even our thoughts and feelings are pressed into a uniform mould and fashioned into sameness. The spirit of authority, law, written and unwritten, tradition and custom force us into a common groove and make of man a will-less automaton without independence or individuality. This moral and intellectual bondage is more compelling than any physical coercion, more devastating to our manhood and development. All of us are its victims, and only the exceptionally strong succeed in breaking its chains, and that only partly.

The authority of the past and of the present dictates not only our behaviour but dominates our very minds and souls, and is continuously at work to stifle every symptom of nonconformity, of independent attitude and unorthodox opinion. The whole weight of social condemnation comes down upon the head of the man or woman who dares defy conventional codes. Ruthless vengeance is wreaked upon the protestant who refuses to follow the beaten track, or upon the heretic who disbelieves in the accepted formulas. In science and art, in literature, poetry and in painting this spirit compels adaptation and adjustment, resulting in imitation of the established and approved, in uniformity and sameness, in stereotyped expression. But more terribly still is punished nonconformity in actual life, in our everyday relationships and behaviour. The painter and writer may occasionally be forgiven for defiance of custom and precedent because, after all, their rebellion is limited to paper or canvas: it affects only a comparatively small circle. They may be disregarded or labelled cranks who can do little harm, but not so with the man of action who carries his challenge of accepted standards into social life. Not harmless he. He is dangerous by the power of example, by his very presence. His infraction of social canons can be neither ignored nor forgiven. He will be denounced as an enemy of society.

It is for this reason that revolutionary feeling or thought expressed in exotic poetry or masked in high-brow philosophic dissertations may be condoned, may pass the official and unofficial censor, because it is neither accessible to nor understood by the public at large. But give voice to the same dissenting attitude in a popular manner, and immediately you will face the frothing denunciation of all the forces that stand for the preservation of the established.

More vicious and deadening is compulsory compliance than the most virulent poison. Throughout the ages it has been the greatest impediment to man's advance, hedging him in with a thousand prohibitions and taboos, weighting his mind and heart down with outlived canons and codes, thwarting his will with imperatives of thought and feeling, with 'thou shalt' and 'thou shalt not' of behaviour and action. Life, the art of living, has become a dull formula, flat and inert.

Yet so strong is the innate diversity of man's nature that centuries of this stultification have not succeeded in entirely eradicating his originality and uniqueness. True, the great majority have fallen into ruts so deepened by countless feet that they cannot get back to the broad spaces. But some do break away from the beaten track and find the open road where new vistas of beauty and inspiration beckon to heart and spirit. These the world condemns, but little by little it follows their example and lead, and finally it comes up abreast of them. In the meantime those pathfinders have gone much further or died, and then we build monuments to them and glorify the men we have vilified and crucified as we go on crucifying their brothers in spirit, the pioneers of our own day.

Beneath this spirit of intolerance and persecution is the habit of authority: coercion to conform to dominant standards, compulsion – moral and legal – to be and act as others, according to precedent and rule.

But the general view that conformity is a natural trait is entirely false. On the contrary, given the least chance, unimpeded by the mental habits instilled from the very cradle, man evidences uniqueness and originality. Observe children, for instance, and you will see most varied differentiation in manner and attitude, in mental and psychic expression. You will discover an instinctive tendency to individuality and independence, to non-conformity, manifested in open and secret defiance of the will imposed from the outside, in rebellion against the authority of parent and teacher. The whole training and 'education' of the child is a continuous process of stifling and crushing this tendency, the eradication of his distinctive characteristics, of his unlikeness to others, of his personality and originality. Yet even in spite of year-long repression, suppression, and moulding, some originality persists in the child when it reaches maturity, which shows how deep are the springs of individuality. Take any two persons, for example, who have witnessed some tragedy, a big fire, let us say, at the same time and place. Each will tell the story in a different manner, each will be original in his way of relating it and in the impression he will produce, because of his naturally different psychology. But talk to the same two persons on some fundamental social matter, about life and government, for instance, and immediately you hear expressed an exactly similar attitude, the accepted view, the dominant mentality.

Why? Because where man is left free to think and feel for himself, unhindered by precept and rule, and not restrained by the fear of being 'different' and unorthodox, with the unpleasant consequences it involves, he will be independent and free. But the moment the conversation touches matters within the sphere of our social imperatives, one is in the clutches of the taboos and becomes a copy and a parrot.

Life in freedom, in anarchy, will do more than liberate man merely from his present political and economic bondage. That will be only the first step, the preliminary to a truly human existence. Far greater and more significant will be the results of such liberty, its effects upon man's mind, upon his personality. The abolition of the coercive external will, and with it of the fear of authority, will loosen the bonds of moral compulsion no less than of economic and physical. Man's spirit will breathe freely, and that mental emancipation will be the birth of a new culture, of a new humanity. Imperatives and taboos will disappear, and man will begin to be himself, to develop and express his individual tendencies and uniqueness. Instead of 'thou shalt not', the public conscience will say 'thou mayest, taking full responsibility'. That will be a training in human dignity and self-reliance, beginning at home and in school, which will produce a new race with a new attitude to life.

The man of the coming day will see and feel existence on an entirely different plane. Living to him will be an art and a joy. He will cease to consider it as a race where every one must try to become as good a runner as the fastest. He will regard leisure as more important than work, and work will fall into its proper, subordinate place as the means to leisure, to the enjoyment of life.

Life will mean the striving for finer cultural values, the penetration of nature's mysteries, the attainment of higher truth. Free to exercise the limitless possibilities of his mind, to pursue his love of knowledge, to apply his inventive genius, to create, and to soar on the wings of imagination, man will reach his full stature and become man indeed. He will grow and develop according to his nature. He will scorn uniformity, and human diversity will give him increased interest in, and a more satisfying sense of, the richness of being. Life to him will not consist in functioning but in living, and he will attain the greatest kind of freedom man is capable of, freedom in joy.

"That day lies far in the future," you say; "how shall we bring it about?"

Far in the future, maybe; yet perhaps not so far – one cannot tell. At any rate we should always hold our ultimate object in view if we are to remain on the right road. The change I have described will not come overnight; nothing ever does. It will be a gradual development, as everything in nature and social life is. But a logical, necessary, and, I dare say, an inevitable development. Inevitable, because the whole trend of man's growth has been in that direction; even if in zigzags, often losing its way, yet always returning to the right path.

How, then, might it be brought about?

Alexander Berkman speaking in Union Square, New York, on May Day, 1908

Chapter 6

NON-COMMUNIST ANARCHISTS

Before we proceed let me make a short explanation. I owe it to those anarchists who are not communists.

Because you should know that not all anarchists are communists: not all of them believe that communism – social ownership and sharing according to need – would be the best and justest economic arrangement.

I have first explained to you communist anarchism because it is, in my estimation, the most desirable and practical form of society. The communist anarchists hold that only under communist conditions could anarchy prosper, and equal liberty, justice, and well-being be assured to every one without discrimination.

But there are anarchists who do not believe in communism. They can be generally classed as individualists and mutualists.*

All anarchists agree on this fundamental position: that government means injustice and oppression, that it is invasive, enslaving, and the greatest hindrance to man's development and growth. They all believe that freedom can exist only in a society where there is no compulsion of any kind. All anarchists are therefore at one on the basic principle of abolishing government.

---

* The mutualists, though not calling themselves anarchists (probably because the name is so misunderstood) are nevertheless thoroughgoing anarchists, since they disbelieve in government and political authority of any kind.

They disagree mostly on the following points:

First: the manner in which anarchy will come about. The communist anarchists say that only a social revolution can abolish government and establish anarchy, while individualist anarchists and mutualists do not believe in revolution. They think that present society will gradually develop out of government into a non-governmental condition.

Second: individualist anarchists and mutualists believe in individual ownership, as against the communist anarchists who see in the institution of private property one of the main sources of injustice and inequality, of poverty and misery. The individualists and mutualists maintain that liberty means "the right of every one to the product of his toil"; which is true, of course. Liberty does mean that. But the question is not whether one has a right to his product, but whether there is such a thing as an individual product. I have pointed out in preceding chapters that there is no such thing in modern industry: all labour and the products of labour are social. The argument, therefore, about the right of the individual to his product has no practical merit.

I have also shown that exchange of products or commodities cannot be individual or private, unless the profit system is employed. Since the value of a commodity cannot be adequately determined, no barter is equitable. This fact leads, in my opinion, to social ownership and use; that is, to communism, as the most practicable and just economic system.

But, as stated, individualist anarchists and mutualists disagree with the communist anarchists on this point. They assert that the source of economic inequality is monopoly, and they argue that monopoly will disappear with the abolition of government, because it is special privilege – given and protected by government – which makes monopoly possible. Free competition, they claim, would do away with monopoly and its evils.

Individualist anarchists, followers of Stirner and Tucker, as well as Tolstoyan anarchists who believe in non-resistance, have no very clear plan of the economic life under anarchy. The mutualists, on the other hand, propose a definite new economic system. They believe with their teacher, the French philosopher Proudhon, that mutual banking and credit without interest would be the best economic form of a non-government society. According to their theory, free credit, affording everyone opportunity to borrow money without interest, would tend to equalise incomes and reduce profits to a minimum, and would thus eliminate riches as well as poverty. Free credit and competition in the open market, they say, would result in economic equality, while the abolition of government would secure equal freedom. The social life of the mutualist community, as well as of the individualist society, would be based on the sanctity of voluntary agreement, of free contract.

I have given here but the briefest outline of the attitude of individualist anarchists and mutualists. It is not the purpose of this work to treat in detail those anarchist ideas which the author thinks erroneous and impractical. Being a communist anarchist I am interested in submitting to the reader the views that I consider best and soundest. I thought it fair, however, not to leave you in ignorance about the existence of other, non-communist anarchist theories.

Alexander Berkman addresses the crowd in Union Square, New York, in 1914

Chapter 7

WHY REVOLUTION?

Let us return to your question, "How will anarchy come? Can we help bring it about?"

This is a most important point, because in every problem there are two vital things: first, to know clearly just what you want; second, how to attain it.

We already know what we want. We want social conditions wherein all will be free and where each shall have the fullest opportunity to satisfy his needs and aspirations, on the basis of equal liberty for all. In other words, we are striving for the free cooperative commonwealth of communist anarchism.

How will it come about?

We are not prophets, and no one can tell just how a thing will happen. But the world does not exist since yesterday; and man, as a reasonable being, must benefit by the experience of the past.

Now, what is that experience? If you glance over history you will see that the whole life of man has been a struggle for existence. In his primitive state man fought single-handed the wild beasts of the forest, and helplessly he faced hunger, cold, darkness, and storm. Because of his ignorance all the forces of nature were his enemies: they worked evil and destruction to him, and he, alone, was powerless to combat them. But little by little man learned to come together with others of his kind; together they sought safety and security. By joint effort they presently began to turn the energies of nature to their service. Mutual help and cooperation gradually multiplied man's strength and ability till he has succeeded in conquering nature, in applying her forces to his use, in chaining the lightning, bridging oceans, and mastering even the air.

Similarly the primitive man's ignorance and fear made life a continuous struggle of man against man, of family against family, of tribe against tribe, until men realised that by getting together, by joint effort and mutual aid, they could accomplish more than by strife and enmity. Modern science shows that even animals had learned that much in the struggle for existence. Certain kinds survived because they quit fighting each other and lived in herds, and in that way were better able to protect themselves against other beasts. In proportion as men substituted joint effort and cooperation in place of mutual struggle, they advanced, grew out of barbarism, and became civilised. Families which had formerly fought each other to the death combined and formed one common group; groups joined and became tribes, and tribes federated into nations. The nations still stupidly keep on fighting each other, but gradually they are also learning the same lesson, and now they are beginning to look for a way to stop the international slaughter known as war.

Unfortunately in our social life we are yet in a condition of barbarism, destructive and fratricidal: group still combats group, class fights against class. But here also men are beginning to see that it is a senseless and ruinous warfare, that the world is big and rich enough to be enjoyed by all, like the sunshine, and that a united mankind would accomplish more than one divided against itself.

What is called progress is just the realisation of this, a step in that direction.

The whole advance of man consists in the striving for greater safety and peace, for more security and welfare. Man's natural impulse is toward mutual help and joint effort, his most instinctive longing is for liberty and joy. These tendencies seek to express and assert themselves in spite of all obstacles and difficulties. The lesson of the entire history of man is that neither hostile natural forces nor human opposition can hold back his onward march. If I were asked to define civilisation in a single phrase I should say that it is the triumph of man over the powers of darkness, natural and human. The inimical forces of nature we have conquered, but we still have to fight the dark powers of men.

History fails to show a single important social improvement made without meeting the opposition of the dominant powers — the church, government, and capital. Not a step forward but was achieved by breaking down the resistance of the masters. Every advance has cost a bitter struggle. It took many long fights to destroy slavery; it required revolts and uprisings to secure the most fundamental rights for the people; it necessitated rebellions and revolutions to abolish feudalism and serfdom. It needed civil warfare to do away with the absolute power of kings and establish democracies, to conquer more freedom and well-being for the masses. There is not a country on earth, not an epoch in history, where any great social evil was eliminated without a bitter struggle with the powers that be. In recent days it again took revolutions to get rid of Tsardom in Russia, of the Kaiser in Germany, the Sultan in Turkey, the monarchy in China, and so on, in various lands.

There is no record of any government or authority, of any group or class in power having given up its mastery voluntarily. In every instance it required the use of force, or at least the threat of it.

Is it reasonable to assume that authority and wealth will experience a sudden change of heart, and that they will behave differently in the future than they had in the past?

Your common sense will tell you that it is a vain and foolish hope. Government and capital will *fight* to retain power. They do it even today at the least menace to their privileges. They will fight to the death for their existence.

That is why it is no prophecy to foresee that some day it must come to a decisive struggle between the masters of life and the dispossessed classes.

As a matter of fact, that struggle is going on all the time.

There is a continuous warfare between capital and labour. That warfare generally proceeds within so-called legal forms. But even these erupt now and then in violence, as during strikes and lockouts, because the armed fist of government is always at the service of the masters, and that fist gets into action the moment capital feels its profits threatened: then it drops the mask of 'mutual interests' and 'partnership' with labour and resorts to the final argument of every master, to coercion and force.

It is therefore certain that government and capital will not allow themselves to be quietly abolished if they can help it; nor will they miraculously 'disappear' of themselves, as some people pretend to believe. It will require a revolution to get rid of them.

There are those who smile incredulously at the mention of revolution. "Impossible!" they say confidently. So did Louis XVI and Marie Antoinette of France think only a few weeks before they lost their throne, together with their heads. So did the nobility at the court of Tsar Nicholas II believe on the very eve of the upheaval that swept them away. "It doesn't look like revolution," the superficial observer argues. But revolutions have a way of breaking out when it "doesn't look like it." The more far-seeing modern capitalists, however, do not seem willing to take any chances. They know that uprisings and revolutions are possible at any time. That is why the great corporations and big employers of labour, particularly in America, are beginning to introduce new methods calculated to serve as lightning rods against popular disaffection and revolt. They initiate bonuses for their employees, profit sharing, and similar methods designed to make the worker more satisfied and financially interested in the prosperity of his industry. These means may temporarily blind the proletarian to his true interests, but do not believe that the worker will forever remain content with his wage slavery, even if his cage be slightly gilded from time to time. Improving material conditions is no insurance against revolution. On the contrary, the satisfaction of our wants creates new needs, gives birth to new desires and aspirations. That is human nature, and that's what makes improvement and progress possible. Labour's discontent is not to be choked down with an extra piece of bread, even if it be buttered. That is why there is more conscious and active revolt in the industrial centres of better-situated Europe than in backward Asia and Africa. The spirit of man forever yearns for greater comfort and freedom, and it is the masses who are the truest bearers of this incentive to further advancement. The hope of modern plutocracy to forestall revolution by throwing a fatter bone to the toiler now and then is illusory and baseless. The new policies of capital may seem to appease labour for a while, but its onward march cannot be stopped by such makeshifts. The abolition of capitalism is inevitable, in spite of all schemes and resistance, and it will be accomplished only by revolution.

A revolution is similar to the struggle of man against nature. Single-handed he is powerless and cannot succeed; by the aid of his fellow-men he triumphs over all obstacles.

Can the individual worker accomplish anything against the big corporation? Can a small labour union compel the large employer to grant its demands? The capitalist class is organised in its fight against labour. It stands to reason that a revolution can be fought successfully only when the workers are united, when they are organised throughout the land; when the proletariat of all countries will make a joint effort, for capital is international and the masters always combine against labour in every big issue. That is why, for instance, the plutocracy of the whole world turned against the Russian Revolution. As long as the people of Russia meant only to abolish the Tsar, international capital did not interfere: it did not care what political form Russia would have, as long as the government would be bourgeois and capitalistic. But as soon as the Revolution attempted to do away with the system of capitalism, the governments and the bourgeoisie of every land combined to crush it. They saw in it a menace to the continuance of their own mastery.

Keep that well in mind, my friend. Because there are revolutions and revolutions. Some revolutions change only the governmental form by putting in a new set of rulers in place of the old. These are political revolutions, and as such they often meet with little resistance. But a revolution that aims to abolish the entire system of wage slavery must also do away with the power of one class to oppress another. That is, it is not any more a mere change of rulers, of government, not a political revolution, but one that seeks to alter the whole character of society. That would be a social revolution. As such it would have to fight not only government and capitalism, but it would also meet with the opposition of popular ignorance and prejudice, of those who believe in government and capitalism.

How is it then to come about?

Chapter 8.

THE IDEA IS THE THING

Did you ever ask yourself how it happens that government and capitalism continue to exist in spite of all the evil and trouble they are causing in the world?

If you did, then your answer must have been that it is because the people support those institutions, and that they support them because they *believe* in them.

That is the crux of the whole matter: present-day society rests on the belief of the people that it is good and useful. It is founded on the idea of authority and private ownership. It is ideas that maintain conditions. Government and capitalism are the forms in which the popular ideas express themselves. Ideas are the foundation; the institutions are the house built upon it.

A new social structure must have a new foundation, new ideas at its base. However you may change the form of an institution, its character and meaning will remain the same as the foundation on which it is built. Look closely at life and you will perceive the truth of this. There are all kinds and forms of government in the world, but their real nature is the same everywhere, as their effects are the same: it always means authority and obedience.

Now, what makes governments exist? The armies and navies? Yes, but only apparently so. What supports the armies and navies? It is the belief of the people, of the masses, that government is necessary; it is the generally accepted idea of the *need* of government. That is its real and solid foundation. Take that idea or belief away, and no government could last another day.

The same applies to private ownership. The idea that it is right and necessary is the pillar that supports it and gives it security.

Not a single institution exists today but is founded on the popular belief that it is good and beneficial.

Let us take an illustration; the United States, for instance. Ask yourself why revolutionary propaganda has been of so little effect in that country in spite of fifty years of socialist and anarchist effort. Is the American worker not exploited more intensely than labour in other countries? Is political corruption as rampant in any other land? Is the capitalist class in America not the most arbitrary and despotic in the world? True, the worker in the United States is better situated materially than in Europe, but is he not at the same time treated with the utmost brutality and terrorism the moment he shows the least dissatisfaction? Yet the American worker remains loyal to the government and is the first to defend it against criticism. He is still the most devoted champion of the 'grand and noble institutions of the greatest country on earth'. Why? Because he believes that they are his institutions, that he, as sovereign and free citizen, is running them and that he could change them if he so wished. It is his *faith* in the existing order that constitutes its greatest security against revolution. His faith is stupid and unjustified, and some day it will break down and with it American capitalism and despotism. But as long as that faith persists, American plutocracy is safe against revolution.

As men's minds broaden and develop, as they advance to new ideas and lose faith in their former beliefs, institutions begin to change and are ultimately done away with. The people grow to understand that their former views were false, that they were not truth but prejudice and superstition.

In this way many ideas, once held to be true, have come to be regarded as wrong and evil. Thus the ideas of the divine right of kings, of slavery and serfdom. There was a time when the whole world believed those institutions to be right, just, and unchangeable. In the measure that those superstitions and false beliefs were fought by advanced thinkers, they became discredited and lost their hold upon the people, and finally the institutions that incorporated those ideas were abolished. Highbrows will tell you that they had 'outlived their usefulness' and that therefore they 'died.' But how did they 'outlive' their 'usefulness'? To whom were they useful, and how did they 'die'?

We know already that they were useful only to the master class, and that they were done away with by popular uprisings and revolutions.

Why did not old and effete institutions 'disappear' and die off in a peaceful manner?

For two reasons: first, because some people think faster than others. So that it happens that a minority in a given place advance in their views quicker than the rest. The more that minority will become imbued with the new ideas, the more convinced of their truth, and the stronger they will feel themselves, the sooner they will try to realise their ideas; and that is usually before the majority have come to see the new light. So that the minority have to struggle against the majority who still cling to the old views and conditions.

Second, the resistance of those who hold power. It makes no difference whether it is the church, the king, or kaiser, a democratic government or a dictatorship, a republic or an autocracy – those in authority will fight desperately to retain it as long as they can hope for the least chance of success. And the more aid they get from the slower-thinking majority the better the fight they can put up. Hence the fury of revolt and revolution.

The desperation of the masses, their hatred of those responsible for their misery, and the determination of the lords of life to hold on to their privileges and rule combine to produce the violence of popular uprisings and rebellions.

But blind rebellion without definite object and purpose is not revolution. Revolution is rebellion become conscious of its aims. Revolution is *social* when it strives for a *fundamental* change. As the foundation of life is economics, the social revolution means the reorganisation of the industrial, economic life of the country and consequently also of the entire structure of society.

But we have seen that the social structure rests on the basis of *ideas*, which implies that changing the structure presupposes changed ideas. In other words, social ideas must change *first* before a new social structure can be built.

The social revolution, therefore, is not an accident, not a sudden happening. There is nothing sudden about it, for ideas don't change suddenly. They grow slowly, gradually, like the plant or flower. Hence the social revolution is a result, a development, which means that it is revolutionary. It develops to the point when considerable numbers of people have embraced the new ideas and are determined to put them into practice. When they attempt to do so and meet with opposition, then the slow, quiet, and peaceful social evolution becomes quick, militant, and violent. Evolution becomes revolution.

Bear in mind, then, that evolution and revolution are *not* two separate and different things. Still less are they opposites, as some people wrongly believe. Revolution is merely the boiling point of evolution.

Because revolution is evolution at its boiling point you cannot 'make' a real revolution any more than you can hasten the boiling of a tea kettle. It is the fire underneath that makes it boil: how quickly it will come to the boiling point will depend on how strong the fire is.

The economic and political conditions of a country are the fire under the evolutionary pot. The worse the oppression, the greater the dissatisfaction of the people, the stronger the flame. This explains why the fires of social revolution swept Russia, the most tyrannous and backward country, instead of America where industrial development has almost reached its highest point – and that in spite of all the learned demonstration of Karl Marx to the contrary.

We see, then, that revolutions, though they cannot be made, can be hastened by certain factors; namely, by pressure from above: by more intense political and economical oppression; and by pressure from below:

by greater enlightenment and agitation. These spread the ideas; they further evolution and thereby also the coming of revolution.

But pressure from above, though hastening revolution, may also cause its failure, because such revolution is apt to break out before the evolutionary process has been sufficiently advanced. Coming prematurely, as it were, it will fizzle out in mere rebellion; that is, without clear, conscious aim and purpose. At best, rebellion can secure only some temporary alleviation; the real causes of the strife, however, remain intact and continue to operate to the same effect, to cause further dissatisfaction and rebellion.

Summing up what I have said about revolution, we must come to the conclusion that:

1. social revolution is one that entirely changes the foundation of society, its political, economic, and social character;
2. such a change must first take place in the ideas and opinions of the people, in the minds of men;
3. oppression and misery may hasten revolution, but may *thereby* also turn it into failure, because lack of evolutionary preparation will make real accomplishment impossible;
4. only that revolution can be fundamental, social, and successful which will be the expression of a basic change of ideas and opinions.

From this it obviously follows that the social revolution must be prepared. Prepared in the sense of furthering the evolutionary process, of enlightening the people about the evils of present-day society and convincing them of the desirability and possibility, of the justice and practicability of a social life based on liberty; prepared, moreover, by making the masses realise very clearly just what they need and how to bring it about.

Such preparation is not only an absolutely necessary preliminary step. Therein lies also the safety of the revolution, the only guarantee of its accomplishing its objects.

It has been the fate of most revolutions – as a result of lack of preparation – to be sidetracked from their main purpose, to be misused and led into blind alleys. Russia is the best recent illustration of it. The

February Revolution, which sought to do away with the autocracy, was
entirely successful. The people knew exactly what they wanted; namely the
abolition of Tsardom. All the machinations of politicians, all the oratory
and schemes of the Lvovs and Miliukovs – the 'liberal' leaders of those
days could not save the Romanov régime in the face of the intelligent and
conscious will of the people. It was this clear understanding of its aims
which made the February Revolution a complete success, with, mind you,
almost no bloodshed.

Furthermore, neither appeals nor threats by the Provisional Government
could avail against the determination of the people to end the war. The
armies left the fronts and thus terminated the matter by their own direct
action. The will of a people conscious of their objects always conquers.

It was the will of the people again, their resolute aim to get hold of the
soil, which secured for the peasant the land he needed. Similarly the city
workers, as repeatedly mentioned before, possessed themselves of the
factories and the machinery of production.

So far the Russian Revolution was a complete success. But at the point
where the masses lacked the consciousness of definite purpose, defeat
began. That is always the moment when politicians and political parties step
in to exploit the revolution for their own uses or to experiment their
theories upon it. This happened in Russia, as in many previous revolutions.
The people fought the good fight – the political parties fought over the
spoils to the detriment of the revolution and to the ruin of the people.

This is, then, what took place in Russia. The peasant, having secured the
land, did not have the tools and machinery he needed. The worker, having
taken possession of the machinery and factories, did not know how to
handle them to accomplish his aims. In other words, he did not have the
experience necessary to organise production and he could not manage the
distribution of the things he was producing.

His own efforts – the worker's, the peasant's, the soldier's – had done
away with Tsardom, paralysed the government, stopped the war, and
abolished private ownership of land and machinery. For that he was
prepared by years of revolutionary education and agitation. But for no

more than that. And because he was prepared for no more, where his knowledge ceased and definite purpose was lacking, there stepped in the political party and took affairs out of the hands of the masses who had made the revolution. Politics replaced economic reconstruction and thereby sounded the death knell of the social revolution; for people live by bread, by economics, not by politics.

Food and supplies are not created by decree of party or government. Legislative edicts don't till the soil; laws can't turn the wheels of industry. Dissatisfaction, strife, and famine came upon the heels of government coercion and dictatorship. Again, as always, politics and authority proved the swamp in which the revolutionary fires became extinguished.

Let us learn this most vital lesson: thorough understanding by the masses of the true aims of revolution means success. Carrying out their conscious will by their own efforts guarantees the right development of the new life. On the other hand, lack of this understanding and of preparation means certain defeat, either at the hands of reaction or by the experimental theories of would-be political party friends.

Let us prepare, then.

Alexander Berkman

Chapter 9

PREPARATION

"Prepare for revolution!" exclaims your friend; "is that possible?"

Yes. Not only is it possible but absolutely necessary.

"Do you refer to secret preparations, armed bands, and men to lead the fight?" you ask.

No, my friend, not that at all.

If the social revolution meant only street battles and barricades, then the preparations you have in mind would be the thing. But revolution does not signify that; at least the fighting phase of it is the smallest and least important part.

The truth is, in modern times revolution does not mean barricades any more. These belong to the past. The social revolution is a far different and more essential matter. It involves the reorganisation of the entire life of society. You will agree that this is certainly not to be accomplished by mere fighting.

Of course, the obstacles in the path of the social reconstruction have to be removed. That is to say, the means of that reconstruction must be secured by the masses. Those means are at present in the hands of government and capitalism, and these will resist every effort to deprive them of their power and possessions. That resistance will involve a fight. But remember that the fight is not the main thing, is not the object, not the revolution. It is only the preface, the preliminary to it.

It is very necessary that you get this straight. Most people have very confused notions about revolution. To them it means just fighting, smashing things, destroying. It is the same as if rolling up your sleeves for work should be considered as the work itself that you have to do. The fighting part of revolution is merely the rolling up of your sleeves. The real, actual task is ahead.

What is that task?

"The destruction of the existing conditions," you reply.

True. But *conditions* are not destroyed by breaking and smashing things. You can't destroy wage slavery by wrecking the machinery in mills and factories, can you? You won't destroy government by setting fire to the White House.

To think of revolution in terms of violence and destruction is to misinterpret and falsify the whole idea of it. In practical application such a conception is bound to lead to disastrous results.

When a great thinker, like the famous anarchist Bakunin, speaks of revolution as destruction, he has in mind the ideas of authority and obedience which are to be destroyed. It is for this reason that he said that destruction means construction, for to destroy a false belief is indeed most constructive work.

But the average man, and too often even the revolutionist, thoughtlessly talks of revolution as being exclusively destructive in the physical sense of the word. That is a wrong and dangerous view. The sooner we get rid of it the better.

Revolution, and particularly the social revolution, is *not destruction but construction*. This cannot be sufficiently emphasised, and unless we clearly realise it, revolution will remain only destructive and thereby always a failure. Naturally revolution is accompanied by violence, but you might as well say that building a new house in place of an old one is destructive because you have first to tear down the old one. Revolution is the culminating point of a certain evolutionary process: it begins with a violent upheaval. It is the rolling up of your sleeves preparatory to *starting the actual work*.

Indeed, consider what the social revolution is to do, what it is to accomplish, and you will perceive that it comes not to destroy but to build.

What, really, is there to destroy?

The wealth of the rich? Nay, that is something we want the whole of society to enjoy.

The land, the fields, the coal mines, the railroads, factories, mills, and shops? These we want not to destroy but to make useful to the entire people.

The telegraphs, telephones, the means of communication and distribution – do we want to destroy them? No, we want them to serve the needs of all.

What, then, is the social revolution to destroy? It is to take over things for the general benefit, not to destroy them. It is to reorganise conditions for the public welfare.

Not to destroy is the aim of the revolution, but to reconstruct and rebuild.

It is for this that preparation is needed, because the social revolution is not the Biblical Messiah who is to accomplish his mission by simple edict or order. Revolution works with the hands and brains of men. And these have to understand the objects of the revolution so as to be able to carry them out. They will have to know what they want and how to achieve it. The way to achieve it will be pointed by the objects to be attained. For the end determines the means, just as you have to sow a particular seed to grow the thing you need.

What, then, must the preparation for the social revolution be?

If your object is to secure liberty, you must learn to do without authority and compulsion. If you intend to live in peace and harmony with your fellow-men, you and they should cultivate brotherhood and respect for each other. If you want to work together with them for your mutual benefit, you must practice co-operation. The social revolution means much more than the reorganisation of conditions only: it means the establishment of new human values and social relationships, a changed attitude of man to man, as of one free and independent to his equal; it means a different spirit in individual and collective life, and that spirit cannot be born overnight. It is a spirit to be cultivated, to be nurtured and reared, as the most delicate flower is, for indeed it is the flower of a new and beautiful existence.

Do not dupe yourself with the silly notion that 'things will arrange themselves.' Nothing ever arranges itself, least of all in human relations. It is men who do the arranging, and they do it according to their attitude and understanding of things.

New situations and changed conditions make us feel, think, and act in a different manner. But the new conditions themselves come about only as a result of new feelings and ideas. The social revolution is such a new condition. We must learn to think differently before the revolution can come. That alone can bring the revolution.

We must learn to think differently about government and authority, for as long as we think and act as we do today, there will be intolerance, persecution, and oppression, even when organised government is abolished. We must learn to respect the humanity of our fellow-man, not to invade him or coerce him, to consider his liberty as sacred as our own; to respect his freedom and his personality, to forswear compulsion in any form: to understand that the cure for the evils of liberty is more liberty, that liberty is the mother of order.

And furthermore we must learn that equality means equal opportunity, that monopoly is the denial of it, and that only brotherhood secures equality. We can learn this only by freeing ourselves from the false ideas of capitalism and of property, of mine and thine, of the narrow conception of ownership.

By learning this we shall grow into the spirit of true liberty and solidarity, and know that free association is the soul of every achievement. We shall then realise that the social revolution is the work of co-operation, of solidaric purpose, of mutual effort.

Maybe you think this too slow a process, a work that will take too long. Yes, I must admit that it is a difficult task. But ask yourself if it is better to build your new house quickly and badly and have it break down over your head, rather than to do it efficiently, even if it requires longer and harder work.

Remember that the social revolution represents the liberty and welfare of the whole of mankind, that the complete and final emancipation of labour depends upon it. Consider also that if the work is badly done, all the effort and suffering involved in it will be for nothing and perhaps even worse than for nothing, because making a botch job of revolution means putting a new tyranny in place of the old, and new tyrannies, because they are new, have a new lease on life. It means forging new chains which are stronger than the old.

Consider also that the social revolution we have in mind is to accomplish the work that many generations of men have been labouring to achieve, for the whole history of man has been a struggle of liberty against servitude, of social well-being against poverty and wretchedness, of justice against iniquity. What we call progress has been a painful but continuous march in the direction of limiting authority and the power of government and increasing the rights and liberties of the individual, of the masses. It has been a struggle that has taken thousands of years. The reason that it took such a long time – and is not ended yet – is because people did not know what the real trouble was: they fought against this and for that, they changed kings and formed new governments, they put out one ruler only to set up another, they drove away a 'foreign' oppressor only to suffer the yoke of a native one, they abolished one form of tyranny, such as the Tsars, and submitted to that of a party dictatorship, and always and ever they shed their blood and heroically sacrificed their lives in the hope of securing liberty and welfare.

But they secured only new masters, because however desperately and nobly they fought, they never touched the *real source* of trouble, the *principle of authority and government*. They did not know that *that* was the fountainhead of enslavement and oppression, and therefore they never succeeded in gaining liberty.

But now we understand that true liberty is not a matter of changing kings or rulers. We know that the whole system of master and slave must go, that the entire social scheme is wrong, that government and compulsion must be abolished, that the very foundations of authority and monopoly must be uprooted. Do you still think any kind of preparation for such a great task can be too difficult?

Let us, then, fully realise how important it is to prepare for the social revolution, and to prepare for it in the right way.

"But what is the right way?" you demand. "And who is to prepare?"

Who is to prepare? First of all, you and I – those who are interested in the success of the revolution, those who want to help bring it about. And you and I means every man and woman; at least every decent man and woman, every one who hates oppression and loves liberty, every one who cannot endure the misery and injustice which fill the world today.

And above all it is those who suffer most from existing conditions, from wage slavery, subjection, and indignity.

"The workers, of course," you say.

Yes, the workers. As the worst victims of present institutions, it is to their own interest to abolish them. It has been truly said that "the emancipation of the workers must be accomplished by the workers themselves," for no other social class will do it for them. Yet labour's emancipation means at the same time the redemption of the whole of society, and that is why some people speak of labour's 'historic mission' to bring about the better day.

But 'mission' is the wrong word. It suggests a duty or task imposed on one from the outside, by some external power. It is a false and misleading conception, essentially a religious, metaphysical sentiment. Indeed, if the emancipation of labour is a 'historic mission', then history will see to it that it is carried out no matter what we may think, feel, or do about it. This attitude makes human effort unnecessary, superfluous; because 'what must be will be'. Such a fatalistic notion is destructive to all initiative and the exercise of one's mind and will.

It is a dangerous and harmful idea. There is no power outside of man which can free him, none which can charge him with any 'mission'. Neither heaven nor history can do it. History is the story of what has happened. It can teach a lesson but not impose a task. It is not the 'mission' but the *interest* of the proletariat to emancipate itself from bondage. If labour does not consciously and actively strive for it, it will never 'happen'. It is necessary to free ourselves from the stupid and false notion of 'historic missions.' It is only by growing to a true realisation of their present position, by visualising their possibilities and powers, by learning unity and co-operation, and practicing them, that the masses can attain freedom. In achieving that they will also have liberated the rest of mankind.

Because of this the proletarian struggle is the concern of every one, and all sincere men and women should therefore be at the service of labour in its great task. Indeed, though only the toilers can accomplish the work of emancipation they need the aid of other social groups. For you must remember that the revolution faces the difficult problem of reorganising the world and building a new civilisation – a work that will require the greatest revolutionary integrity and the intelligent co-operation of all well-meaning and liberty-loving elements. We already know that the social revolution is not a matter of abolishing capitalism only. We might turn out capitalism, as feudalism was got rid of, and still remain slaves as before. Instead of being, as now, the bondmen of private monopoly we might become the servants of state capitalism, as has happened to the people in Russia, for instance, and as conditions are developing in Italy and other lands.

The social revolution, it must never be forgotten, is not to alter one form of subjection for another, but is to do away with everything that can enslave and oppress you.

A political revolution may be carried to a successful issue by a conspirative minority, putting one ruling faction in place of another. But the social revolution is not a mere political change: it is a fundamental economic, ethical, and cultural transformation. A conspirative minority or political party undertaking such a work must meet with the active and passive opposition of the great majority and therefore degenerate into a system of dictatorship and terror.

In the face of a hostile majority the social revolution is doomed to failure from its very beginning. It means, then, that the first preparatory work of the revolution consists in winning over the masses at large in favour of the revolution and its objects, winning them over, at least, to the extent of neutralising them, of turning them from active enemies to passive sympathisers, so that they may not fight against the revolution even if they do not fight for it.

The actual, positive work of the social revolution must, of course, be carried on by the toilers themselves, by the labouring people. And here let us bear in mind that it is not only the factory hand who belongs to labour but the farm worker as well. Some radicals are inclined to lay too much stress on the industrial proletariat, almost ignoring the existence of the agricultural toiler. Yet what could the factory worker accomplish without the farmer? Agriculture is the primal source of life, and the city would starve but for the country. It is idle to compare the industrial worker with the farm labourer or discuss their relative value. Neither can do without the other; both are equally important in the scheme of life and equally so in the revolution and the building of a new society.

It is true that revolution first breaks out in industrial localities rather than in agricultural. This is natural, since these are greater centres of labouring population and therefore also of popular dissatisfaction. But if the industrial proletariat is the advance-guard of revolution, then the farm labourer is its backbone. If the latter is weak or broken, the advance-guard, the revolution itself, is lost.

Therefore, the work of the social revolution lies in the hands of *both* the industrial worker and the farm labourer. Unfortunately it must be admitted that there is too little understanding and almost no friendship or direct co-operation between the two. Worse than that – and no doubt the result of it – there is a certain dislike and antagonism between the proletarians of field and factory. The city man has too little appreciation of the hard and exhausting toil of the farmer. The latter instinctively resents it; moreover, unfamiliar with the strenuous and often dangerous labour of the factory, the farmer is apt to look upon the city worker as an idler. A closer approach and better understanding between the two is absolutely vital. Capitalism thrives not so much on division of work as on the division of the workers. It seeks to incite race against race, the factory hand against the farmer, the labourer against the skilled man, the workers of one country against those of another. The strength of the exploiting class lies in disunited, divided labour. But the social revolution requires the *unity* of the toiling masses, and first of all the co-operation of the factory-proletarian with his brother in the field.

A nearer approach between the two is an important step in preparation for the social revolution. Actual contact between them is of prime necessity. Joint councils, exchange of delegates, a system of cooperatives, and other similar methods, would tend to form a closer bond and better understanding between the worker and farmer.

But it is not only the co-operation of the factory proletarian with the farm labourer which is necessary for the revolution. There is another element absolutely needed in its constructive work. It is the trained mind of the professional man.

Do not make the mistake of thinking that the world has been built with hands only. It has also required brains. Similarly does the revolution need *both* the man of brawn and the man of brain. Many people imagine that the manual worker alone can do the entire work of society. It is a false idea, a very grave error that can bring no end of harm. In fact, this conception has worked great evil on previous occasions, and there is good reason to fear that it may defeat the best efforts of the revolution.

The working class consists of the industrial wage earners and the agricultural toilers. But the workers require the services of the professional elements, of the industrial organiser, the electrical and mechanical engineer, the technical specialist, the scientist, inventor, chemist, the educator, doctor, and surgeon. In short, the proletariat absolutely needs the aid of certain professional elements without whose co-operation no productive labour is possible.

Most of those professional men in reality also belong to the proletariat. They are the intellectual proletariat, the proletariat of brain. It is clear that it makes no difference whether one earns his living with his hands or with his head. As a matter of fact, no work is done *only* with the hands or only with the brain. The application of both is required in every kind of effort. The carpenter, for instance, must estimate, measure, and figure in the course of his task: he must use both hand and brain. Similarly the architect must think out his plan before it can be drawn on paper and put to practical use.

"But only labour can produce," your friend objects; "brain work is not productive."

Wrong, my friend. Neither manual labour nor brain work can produce anything *alone*. It requires both, working together, to create something. The bricklayer and mason can't build the factory without the architect's plans, nor can the architect erect a bridge without the iron and steel worker. Neither can produce alone. But both together can accomplish wonders.

Furthermore, do not fall into the error of believing that only productive labour counts. There is much work that is not directly productive, but which is useful and even absolutely necessary to our existence and comfort, and therefore just as important as productive labour.

Take the railroad engineer and contractor, for instance. They are not producers, but they are essential factors in the system of production. Without the railroads and other means of transport and communication we could manage neither production nor distribution.

Production and distribution are the two points of the same life pole. The labour required for the one is as important as that needed for the other.

What I said above applies to numerous phases of human effort which, though themselves not directly productive, play a vital part in the manifold processes of our economic and social life. The man of science, the educator, the physician and surgeon are not productive in the industrial sense of the word. But their work is absolutely necessary to our life and welfare. Civilised society could not exist without them.

It is therefore evident that useful work is equally important whether it be that of brain or of brawn, manual or mental. Nor does it matter whether it is a salary or wages which one receives, whether he is paid much or little, or what his political or other opinions might be.

All the elements that can contribute useful work to the general welfare are needed in the revolution for the building of the new life. No revolution can succeed without their solidaric co-operation, and the sooner we understand this the better. The reconstruction of society involves the reorganisation of industry, the proper functioning of production, the management of distribution, and numerous other social, educational, and cultural efforts to transform present-day wage slavery and servitude into a life of liberty and well-being. Only by working hand in hand will the proletariat of brain and brawn be able to solve those problems.

It is most regrettable that there exists a spirit of unfriendliness, even of enmity, between the manual and intellectual workers. That feeling is rooted in lack of understanding, in prejudice and narrow-mindedness on both sides. It is sad to admit that there is a tendency in certain labour circles, even among some socialists and anarchists, to antagonise the workers against the members of the intellectual proletariat. Such an attitude is stupid and criminal, because it can only work evil to the growth and development of the social revolution. It was one of the fatal mistakes of the Bolsheviks during the first phases of the Russian Revolution that they deliberately set the wage earners against the professional classes, to such an extent indeed that friendly co-operation became impossible. A direct result of that policy was the breaking down of industry for lack of intelligent direction, as well as the almost total suspension of railroad communication because that was no trained management. Seeing Russia facing economic shipwreck, Lenin decided that the factory worker and farmer alone could not carry on the industrial and agricultural life of the country, and that the aid of the professional elements was necessary. He introduced a new system to induce the technical men to help in the work of reconstruction. But almost too late came the change, for the years of mutual hating and hounding had created such a gulf between the manual worker and his intellectual brother that common understanding and co-operation were made exceptionally difficult. It has taken Russia years of heroic effort to undo, to some extent, the effects of that fratricidal war.

Let us learn this valuable lesson from the Russian experiment.

"But professional men belong to the middle classes," you object, "and they are bourgeois-minded."

True, men of the professions generally have a bourgeois attitude toward things; but are not most working men also bourgeois-minded? It merely means that both are steeped in authoritarian and capitalistic prejudices. It is just these that must be eradicated by enlightening and educating the people, be they manual or brain workers. That is the first step in preparation for the social revolution.

But it is not true that professional men, as such, necessarily belong to the middle classes.

The real interests of the so-called intellectuals are with the workers rather than with the masters. To be sure, most of them do not realise that. But no more does the comparatively highly-paid railroad conductor or locomotive engineer feel himself a member of the working class. By his income and attitude he also belongs to the bourgeoisie. But it is not income or feeling that determines to what social class a person belongs. If the street beggar should fancy himself a millionaire, would he thereby be one? What one imagines himself to be does not alter his actual situation. And the actual situation is that whoever has to sell his labour is an employee, a salaried dependent, a wage earner, and as such his true interests are those of employees and he belongs to the working class.

As a matter of fact, the intellectual proletarian is even more subject to his capitalistic master than the man with pick and shovel. The latter can easily change his place of employment. If he does not care to work for a certain boss he can look for another. The intellectual proletarian, on the other hand, is much more dependent on his particular job. His sphere of exertion is more limited. Not skilled in any trade and physically incapable of serving as a day labourer, he is (as a rule) confined to the comparatively narrow field of architecture, engineering, journalism, or similar work. This puts him more at the mercy of his employer and therefore also inclines him to side with the latter as against his more independent fellow-worker at the bench.

But whatever the attitude of the salaried and dependent intellectual, he belongs to the proletarian class. Yet it is entirely false to maintain that the intellectuals always side with the masters as against the workers. "Generally they do," I hear some radical fanatic interject. And the workers? Do *they* not, generally, support the masters and the system of capitalism? Could that system continue but for their support? It would be wrong to argue from that, however, that the workers consciously join hands with their exploiters. No more is it true of the intellectuals. If the majority of the latter stand by the ruling class it is because of social ignorance, because they do not understand their own best interests, for all their 'intellectuality'. Just so the great masses of labour, similarly unaware of their true interests, aid the masters against their fellow-workers, sometimes even in the same trade and factory, not to speak of their lack of national and international solidarity. It merely proves that the one as the other, the manual worker no less than the brain proletarian, needs enlightenment.

In justice to the intellectuals let us not forget that their best representatives have always sided with the oppressed. They have advocated liberty and emancipation, and often they were the first to voice the deepest aspirations of the toiling masses. In the struggle for freedom they have frequently fought on the barricades shoulder to shoulder with the workers and died championing their cause.

We need not look far for proof of this. It is a familiar fact that every progressive, radical, and revolutionary movement within the past hundred years has been inspired, mentally and spiritually, by the efforts of the finest element of the intellectual classes. The initiators and organisers of the revolutionary movement in Russia, for instance, dating back a century, were intellectuals, men and women of non-proletarian origin and station. Nor was their love of freedom merely theoretical. Literally thousands of them consecrated their knowledge and experience, and dedicated their lives, to the service of the masses. Not a land exists but where such noble men and women have testified to their solidarity with the disinherited by exposing themselves to the wrath and persecution of their own class and joining hands with the downtrodden. Recent history, as well as the past, is full of such examples. Who were the Garibaldis, the Kossuths, the Liebknechts, Rosa Luxemburgs, the Landauers, the Lenins, and Trotskys but intellectuals of the middle classes who gave themselves to the proletariat? The history of every country and of every revolution shines with their unselfish devotion to liberty and labour.

Let us bear these facts in mind and not be blinded by fanatical prejudice and baseless antagonism. The intellectual has done labour great service in the past. It will depend on the attitude of the workers toward him as to what share he will be able and willing to contribute to the preparation and realisation of the social revolution.

Chapter 10.

ORGANISATION OF LABOUR FOR THE SOCIAL REVOLUTION

Proper preparation, as suggested in the preceding pages, will greatly lighten the task of the social revolution and assure its healthy development and functioning.

Now, what will be the main functions of the revolution?

Every country has its specific conditions, its own psychology, habits, and traditions, and the process of revolution will naturally reflect the peculiarities of every land and its people. But fundamentally all countries are alike in their social (rather anti-social) character: whatever the political forms or economic conditions, they are all built on invasive authority, on monopoly, on the exploitation of labour. The main task of the social revolution is therefore essentially the same everywhere: the abolition of government and of economic inequality, and the socialisation of the means of production and distribution.

Production, distribution, and communication are the basic sources of existence; upon them rests the power of coercive authority and capital. Deprived of that power, governors and rulers become just ordinary men, like you and me, common citizens among millions of others. To accomplish that is consequently the primal and most vital function of the social revolution.

We know that revolution begins with street disturbances and outbreaks: it is the initial phase which involves force and violence. But that is merely the spectacular prologue of the real revolution. The age long misery and indignity suffered by the masses burst into disorder and tumult, the humiliation and injustice meekly borne for decades find vent in acts of fury and destruction. That is inevitable, and it is solely the master class which is responsible for this preliminary character of revolution. For it is even more true socially than individually that "whoever sows the wind will reap the whirlwind": the greater the oppression and wretchedness to which the masses had been made to submit, the fiercer will rage the social storm. All history proves it, but the lords of life have never harkened to its warning voice.

This phase of the revolution is of short duration. It is usually followed by the more conscious, yet still spontaneous, destruction of the citadels of authority, the visible symbols of organised violence and brutality: jails, police stations, and other government buildings are attacked, the prisoners liberated, legal documents destroyed. It is the manifestation of instinctive popular justice. Thus one of the first gestures of the French Revolution was the demolition of the Bastille. Similarly in Russia prisons were stormed and the prisoners released at the very outset of the Revolution. The wholesome intuition of the people justly sees in prisoners social unfortunates, victims of conditions, and sympathises with them as such. The masses regard the courts and their records as instruments of class injustice, and these are destroyed at the beginning of the revolution, and quite properly so.

But this stage passes quickly: the people's ire is soon spent. Simultaneously the revolution begins its constructive work.

"Do you really think that reconstruction could start so soon?" you ask.

My friend, it must begin immediately. In fact, the more enlightened the masses have become, the clearer the workers realise their aims, and the better they are prepared to carry them out, the less destructive the revolution will be, and the quicker and more effectively will begin the work of reconstruction.

"Are you not too hopeful?"

No, I don't think so. I am convinced that the social revolution will not 'just happen'. It will have to be prepared, organised. Yes, indeed, organised-just as a strike is organised. In truth, it will be a strike, the strike of the united workers of an entire country – *a general strike.*

Let us pause and consider this.

How do you imagine a revolution could be fought in these days of armoured tanks, poison gas, and military planes? Do you believe that the unarmed masses and their barricades could withstand high-power artillery and bombs thrown upon them from flying machines? Could labour fight the military forces of government and capital?

It's ridiculous on the face of it, isn't it? And no less ridiculous is the suggestion that the workers should form their own regiments, 'shock troops', or a 'red front', as the communist parties advise you to do. Will such proletarian bodies ever be able to stand up against the trained armies of the government and the private troops of capital? Will they have the least chance?

Such a proposition needs only to be stated to be seen in all its impossible folly. It would simply mean sending thousands of workers to certain death.

It is time to have done with this obsolete idea of revolution. Nowadays government and capital are too well organised in a military way for the workers ever to be able to cope with them. It would be criminal to attempt it, insanity even to think of it.

The strength of labour is not on the field of battle. It is in the shop, in the mine and factory. There lies its power that no army in the world can defeat, no human agency conquer.

In other words, the social revolution can take place only by means of the *general strike.* The general strike, rightly understood and thoroughly carried out, is the social revolution. Of this the British Government became aware much quicker than the workers when the General Strike was declared in England in May, 1926. "It means revolution," the Government said, in effect, to the strike leaders. With all their armies and navies the authorities were powerless in the face of the situation. You can shoot people to death but you can't shoot them to work. The labour leaders themselves were frightened at the thought that the General Strike actually implied revolution.

British capital and government won the strike – not by the strength of arms, but because of the lack of intelligence and courage on the part of the labour leaders and because the English workers were not prepared for the consequences of the General Strike. As a matter of fact, the idea was quite new to them. They had never before been interested in it, never studied its significance and potentialities. It is safe to say that a similar situation in France would have developed quite differently, because in that country the toilers have for years been familiar with the General Strike as a revolutionary proletarian weapon.

It is most important that we realise that the General Strike is the only possibility of social revolution. In the past the General Strike has been propagated in various countries without sufficient emphasis that its real meaning is revolution, that it is the only practical way to it. It is time for us to learn this, and when we do so the social revolution will cease to be a vague, unknown quantity. It will become an actuality, a definite method and aim, a program whose first step is the taking over of the industries by organised labour.

"I understand now why you said that the social revolution means construction rather than destruction," your friend remarks.

I am glad you do. And if you have followed me so far, you will agree that the matter of taking over the industries is not something that can be left to chance, nor can it be carried out in a haphazard manner. It can be accomplished only in a well-planned, systematic, and organised way. You alone can't do it, nor I, nor any other man, be he worker, Ford, or the Pope of Rome. There is no man nor any body of men that can manage it except the *workers themselves*, for it takes the workers to operate the industries. But even the workers can't do it unless they are organised and *organised just for such an undertaking.*

"But I thought you were an anarchist," interrupts your friend.

I am.

"I've heard that anarchists don't believe in organisation."

I imagine you have, but that's an old argument. Any one who tells you that anarchists don't believe in organisation is talking nonsense.

Organisation is everything, and everything is organisation. The whole of life is organisation, conscious or unconscious. Every nation, every family, why, even every individual is an organisation or organism. Every part of every living thing is organised in such a manner that the whole works in harmony. Otherwise the different organs could not function properly and life could not exist.

But there is organisation and organisation. Capitalist society is so badly organised that its various members suffer: just as when you have pain in some part of you, your whole body aches and you are ill.

There is organisation that is painful because it is ill, and organisation that is joyous because it means health and strength. An organisation is ill or evil when it neglects or suppresses any of its organs or members. In the healthy organism all parts are equally valuable and none is discriminated against. The organisation built on compulsion, which coerces and forces, is bad and unhealthy. The libertarian organisation, formed voluntarily and in which every member is free and equal, is a sound body and can work well. Such an organisation is a free union of equal parts. It is the kind of organisation the anarchists believe in.

Such must be the organisation of the workers if labour is to have a healthy body, one that can operate effectively.

It means, first of all, that not a single member of the organisation or union may with impunity be discriminated against, suppressed or ignored. To do so would be the same as to ignore an aching tooth: you would be sick all over.

In other words, the labour union must be built on the principle of the equal liberty of all its members.

Only when each is a free and independent unit, cooperating with the others from his own choice because of mutual interests, can the whole work successfully and become powerful.

This equality means that it makes no difference what or who the particular worker is: whether he is skilled or unskilled, whether he is mason, carpenter, engineer or day labourer, whether he earn much or little. The interests of *all* are the same; all belong together, and only by standing together can they accomplish their purpose.

It means that the workers in the factory, mill, or mine must be organised as one body; for it is not a question of what particular jobs they hold, what craft or trade they follow, but what their interests are. And their interests are identical, as against the employer and the system of exploitation.

Consider yourself how foolish and inefficient is the present form of labour organisation in which one trade or craft may be on strike while the other branches of the same industry continue at work. Is it not ridiculous that when the street car workers of New York, for instance, quit work, the employees of the subway, the cab and omnibus drivers remain on the job? The main purpose of a strike is to bring about a situation that will compel the employer to give in to the demands of labour. Such a situation can be created only by a complete tie-up of the industry in question, so that a partial strike is merely a waste of labour's time and energy, not to speak of the harmful moral effect of the inevitable defeat.

Think over the strikes in which you yourself have taken part and of others you know of. Did your union ever win a fight unless it was able to compel the employer to give in? But *when* was it able to do so? Only when the boss knew that the workers meant business, that there was no dissent among them, that there was no hesitation and dallying, that they were determined to win, at whatever cost. But particularly when the employer felt himself at the mercy of the union, when he could not operate his factory or mine in the face of the workers' resolute stand, when he could not get scabs or strikebreakers, and when he saw that his interests would suffer more by defying his employees than by granting their demands.

It is clear, then, that you can compel compliance only when you are determined, when your union is strong, when you are well organised, when you are united in such a manner that the boss cannot run his factory against your will. But the employer is usually some big manufacturer or a company that has mills or mines in various places. Suppose it is a coal combine. If it cannot operate its mines in Pennsylvania because of a strike, it will try to make good its losses by continuing mining in Virginia or Colorado and increasing production there. Now, if the miners in those states keep on working while you in Pennsylvania are on strike, the company loses nothing. It may even welcome the strike in order to raise the price of coal on the ground that the supply is short because of your strike. In that way the company not only breaks your strike, but it also influences public opinion against you, because the people foolishly believe that the higher price of coal is really the result of your strike while in fact it is due to the greed of the mine owners. You will lose your strike, and for some time to come you and the workers everywhere will have to pay more for coal, and not only for coal but for all the other necessities of life, because together with the price of coal the general cost of living will go up.

Reflect, then, how stupid is the present union policy to permit the other mines to operate while your mine is on strike. The others remain at work and give financial support to your strike, but don't you see that their aid only helps to break your strike, because they have to keep on working, really scabbing on you, in order to contribute to your strike fund? Can anything be more senseless and criminal?

This holds true of every industry and every strike. Can you wonder that most strikes are lost? That is the case in America as well as in other countries. I have before me the Blue Book just published in England under the title of *Labour Statistics.* The data prove that strikes do not lead to labour victories. The figures for the last eight years are as follows:

	Results in favour of working people	Results in favour of employers
1920	390	507
1921	152	315
1922	111	222
1923	187	183
1924	163	235
1925	154	189
1926	67	126
1927	61	118

Actually, then, almost 60% of the strikes were lost. Incidentally, consider also the loss of working days resulting from strikes, which means no wages. The total number of workdays lost by English labour in 1912 was 40,890,000, which is almost equal to the lives of 2,000 men, allotting to each 60 years. In 1919 the number of workdays lost was 34,969,000; in 1920, 26,568,000; in 1921, 85,872,000; in 1926, as a result of the general strike, 162,233,000 days. These figures do not include time and wages lost through unemployment.

It doesn't take much arithmetic to see that strikes as at present conducted don't pay, that the labour unions are not the winners in industrial disputes.

This does not mean, however, that strikes serve no purpose. On the contrary, they are of great value: they teach the worker the vital need of co-operation, of standing shoulder to shoulder with his fellows and unitedly fighting in the common cause. Strikes train him in the class struggle and develop his spirit of joint effort, of resistance to the masters, of solidarity and responsibility. In this sense even an unsuccessful strike is not a complete loss. Through it the toilers learn that 'an injury to one is the concern of all', the practical wisdom that embodies the deepest meaning of the proletarian struggle. This does not relate only to the daily battle for material betterment, but equally so to everything pertaining to the worker and his existence, and particularly to matters where justice and liberty are involved.

It is one of the most inspiring things to see the masses roused in behalf of social justice, whomever the case at issue may concern. For, indeed, it is the concern of all of us, in the truest and deepest sense. The more labour becomes enlightened and aware of its larger interests, the broader and more universal grow its sympathies, the more world-wide its defence of justice and liberty. It was a manifestation of this understanding when the workers in every country protested against the judicial murder of Sacco and Vanzetti in Massachusetts. Instinctively and consciously the masses throughout the world felt, as did all decent men and women, that it is *their* concern when such a crime is being perpetrated. Unfortunately that protest, as many similar ones, contented itself with mere resolutions. Had organised labour resorted to action, such as a general strike, its demands would not have been ignored, and two of the workers' best friends and noblest of men would not have been sacrificed to the forces of reaction.

Equally important, it would have served as a valuable demonstration of the tremendous power of the proletariat, the power that always conquers when it is unified and resolute. This has been proven on numerous occasions in the past when the determined stand of labour prevented planned legal outrages, as in the case of Haywood, Moyer, and Pettibone, officials of the Western Federation of Miners, whom the coal barons of the State of Idaho had conspired to send to the gallows during the miners' strike of 1905. Again, in 1917, it was the solidarity of the toilers which thwarted the execution of Tom Mooney, in California. The sympathetic attitude of organised labour in America toward Mexico has also till now been an obstacle to the military occupation of that country by the United States Government on behalf of the American oil interests. Similarly in Europe united action by the workers has been successful in repeatedly forcing the authorities to grant amnesty to political prisoners. The Government of England so feared the expressed sympathy of British labour for the Russian Revolution that it was compelled to pretend neutrality. It did not dare openly to aid the counter-revolution in Russia. When the dock workers refused to load food and ammunition intended for the White armies, the English Government resorted to deception. It solemnly assured the workers that the shipments were intended for France. In the course of my work collecting historic material in Russia, in 1920 and 1921, I came into possession of official British documents proving that the shipments had been immediately forwarded from France, by direct orders of the British Government, to the counter-revolutionary generals in the North of Russia who had established there the so-called Tchaikovsky-Miller Government. This incident – one out of many – demonstrates the wholesome fear the powers that be have of the awakening class-consciousness and solidarity of the international proletariat.

The stronger the workers grow in this spirit the more effective will be their struggle for emancipation. Class-consciousness and solidarity must assume national and international proportions before labour can attain its full strength. Wherever there is injustice, wherever persecution and suppression – be it the subjugation of the Philippines, the invasion of Nicaragua, the enslavement of the toilers in the Congo by Belgian exploiters, the oppression of the masses in Egypt, China, Morocco, or India – it is the business of the workers everywhere to raise their voice against all such outrages and demonstrate their solidarity in the common cause of the despoiled and disinherited throughout the world.

Labour is slowly advancing to this social consciousness: strikes and other sympathetic expressions are a valuable manifestation of this spirit. If the greater number of strikes are lost at present, it is because the proletariat is not yet fully aware of its national and international interests, is not organised on the right principles, and does not sufficiently realise the need of world-wide co-operation.

Your daily struggles for better conditions would quickly assume a different character if you were organised in such a manner that when your factory or mine goes on strike, the whole industry should quit work; not gradually but at once, all at the same time. Then the employer would be at your mercy, for what could he do when not a wheel turns in the whole industry? He can get enough strikebreakers for one or a few mills, but an entire industry cannot be supplied with them, nor would he consider it safe or advisable. Moreover, suspension of work in any one industry would immediately affect a large number of others, because modern industry is interwoven. The situation would become the direct concern of the whole country, the public would be aroused and demand a settlement. (At present, when your single factory strikes, no one cares and you may starve as long as you remain quiet.) That settlement would again depend on yourself, on the strength of your organisation. When the bosses would see that you know your power and that you are determined, they'd give in quickly enough or seek a compromise. They would be losing millions every day, the strikers might even sabotage the works and machinery, and the employers would be only too anxious to 'settle', while in a strike of one factory or district they usually welcome the situation, knowing as they do that the chances are all against you.

Reflect therefore how important it is in what manner, on *what principles your union is built,* and how vital labour solidarity and cooperation are in your everyday struggle for better conditions. In unity is your strength, but that unity is non-existent and impossible as long as you are organised on craft lines instead of by industries.

There is nothing more important and urgent than that you and your fellow workers see to it immediately that you change the form of your organisation.

But it is not only the form that must be changed. Your union must become clear about its aims and purposes. The worker should most earnestly consider what he really wants, how he means to achieve it, by what methods. He must learn what his union should be, how it should function, and what it should try to accomplish.

Now, what is the union to accomplish? What should be the arms of a real labour union?

First of all, the purpose of the union is to serve the interests of its members. That is its primary duty. There is no quarrel about that; every working man understands it. If some refuse to join a labour body it is because they are too ignorant to appreciate its great value, in which case they must be enlightened. But generally they decline to belong to the union because they have no faith or are disappointed in it. Most of those who remain away from the union do so because they hear much boasting about the strength of organised labour while they know, often from bitter experience, that it is defeated in almost every important struggle. "Oh, the union," they say scornfully, "it don't amount to anything." To speak quite truthfully, to a certain extent they are right. They see organised capital proclaim the open shop policy and defeat the unions; they see labour leaders sell out strikes and betray the workers; they see the membership, the rank and file, helpless in the political machinations in and out of the union. To be sure, they don't understand why it is so; but they do see the facts, and they turn against the union.

Some again refuse to have anything to do with the union because they had at one time belonged to it, and they know what an insignificant role the individual member, the average worker, plays in the affairs of the organisation. The local leaders, the district and central bodies, the national and international officers, and the chiefs of the American Federation of Labour, in the United States, "run the whole show," they will tell you; "you have nothing to do but vote, and if you object you'll fly out."

Unfortunately they are right. You know how the union is managed. The rank and file have little to say. They have delegated the whole power to the leaders, and these have become the bosses, just as in the larger life of society the people are made to submit to the orders of those who were originally meant to serve them – the government and its agents. Once you do that, the power you have delegated will be used against you and your own interests every time. And then you complain that your leaders 'misuse their power'. No, my friend, they don't misuse it; they only use it, for it is the *use* of power which is itself the worst misuse.

All this has to be changed if you really want to achieve results. In society it has to be changed by taking political power away from your governors, abolishing it altogether. I have shown that political power means authority, oppression, and tyranny, and that it is not political government that we need but rational management of our collective affairs.

Just so in your union you need sensible administration of your business. We know what tremendous power labour has as the creator of all wealth and the supporter of the world. If properly organised and united, the workers could control the situation, be the masters of it. But the strength of the worker is not in the union meeting-hall; it is in the shop and factory, in the mill and mine. It is *there* that he must organise; there, on the job. There he knows what he wants, what his needs are, and it is there that he must concentrate his efforts and his will. Every shop and factory should have its special committee to attend to the wants and requirements of the men, not leaders, but members of the rank and file, from the bench and furnace, to look after the demands and complaints of their fellow employees. Such a committee, being on the spot and constantly under the direction and supervision of the workers, wields no power: it merely carries out instructions. Its members are recalled at will and others selected in their place, according to the need of the moment and the ability required for the task in hand. It is the workers who decide the matters at issue and carry their decisions out through the shop committees.

That is the character and form of organisation that labour needs. Only this form can express its real purpose and will, be its adequate spokesman, and serve its true interests.

These shop and factory committees, combined with similar bodies in other mills and mines, associated locally, regionally, and nationally, would constitute a new type of labour organisation which would be the virile voice of toil and its effective agency. It would have the whole weight and energy of the united workers back of it and would represent a power tremendous in its scope and potentialities.

In the daily struggle of the proletariat such an organisation would be able to achieve victories about which the conservative union, as at present built, cannot even dream. It would enjoy the respect and confidence of the masses, would attract the unorganised and unite the labour forces on the basis of the equality of all workers and their joint interests and aims. It would face the masters with the whole might of the working class back of it, in a new attitude of consciousness and strength. Only then would labour acquire unity and the expression of it assume real significance.

Such a union would soon become something more than a mere defender and protector of the worker. It would gain a vital realisation of the meaning of unity and consequent power, of labour solidarity. The factory and shop would serve as a training camp to develop the worker's understanding of his proper role in life, to cultivate his self-reliance and independence, teach him mutual help and co-operation, and make him conscious of his responsibility. He will learn to decide and act on his own judgment, not leaving it to leaders or politicians to attend to his affairs and look out for his welfare. It will be he who will determine, together with his fellows at the bench, what they want and what methods will best serve their aims, and his committee on the spot would merely carry out instructions. The shop and factory would become the worker's school and college. There he will learn his place in society, his function in industry, and his purpose in life. He will mature as a working man and as a man, and the giant of labour will attain his full stature. He will know and be strong thereby.

Not long will he then be satisfied to remain a wage slave, an employee and dependent on the good will of his master whom his toil supports. He will grow to understand that present economic and social arrangements are wrong and criminal, and he will determine to change them. The shop committee and union will become the field of preparation for a new economic system, for a new social life.

You see, then, how necessary it is that you and I, and every man and woman who has the interests of labour at heart, work toward these objects.

And right here I want to emphasise that it is particularly urgent that the more advanced proletarian, the radical and the revolutionary, reflect upon this more earnestly, for to most of them, even to some anarchists, this is only a pious wish, a distant hope. They fail to realise the transcending importance of efforts in that direction. Yet it is no mere dream. Large numbers of progressive working men are coming to this understanding: the Industrial Workers of the World and the revolutionary anarchist-syndicalists in every country are devoting themselves to this end. It is the most pressing need of the present. It cannot be stressed too much that *only the right organisation of the workers* can accomplish what we are striving for. In it lies the salvation of labour and of the future. Organisation from the bottom up, beginning with the shop and factory, on the foundation of the joint interests of the workers everywhere, irrespective of trade, race, or country, by means of mutual effort and united will, alone can solve the labour question and serve the true emancipation of man.

"You were speaking of the workers taking over the industries," your friend reminds me. "How are they going to do this?"

Yes, I was on the subject when you made that remark about organisation. But it is well that the matter was discussed, because there is nothing more vital in the problems we are examining.

To return to the taking over of the industries. It means not only taking them over, but the running of them by labour. As concerns the taking over, you must consider that the workers are actually now in the industries. The taking over consists in the workers remaining where they are, yet *remaining* not as employees but as the rightful collective possessor.

Grasp this point, my friend. The expropriation of the capitalist class during the social revolution – the taking over of the industries – requires tactics directly the reverse of those you now use in a strike. In the latter you quit work and leave the boss in full possession of the mill, factory, or mine. It is an idiotic proceeding, of course, for you give the master the entire advantage: he can put scabs in your place, and you remain out in the cold.

In expropriating, on the contrary, you *stay* on the job and you put the boss out. He may remain only on equal terms with the rest: a worker among workers.

The labour organisations of a given place take charge of the public utilities, of the means of communication, of production and distribution in their particular locality. That is, the telegraphers, the telephone and electrical workers, the railroad men, and so on, take possession (by means of their revolutionary shop committees) of the workshop, factory, or other establishment. The capitalistic foremen, overseers, and managers are removed from the premises if they resist the change and refuse to co-operate. If willing to participate, they are made to understand that henceforth there are neither masters nor owners: that the factory becomes public property in charge of the union of workers engaged in the industry, all equal partners in the general undertaking.

It is to be expected that the higher officials of large industrial and manufacturing concerns will refuse to co-operate. Thus they eliminate themselves. Their place must be taken by workers previously prepared for the job. That is why I have emphasised the utmost importance of industrial preparation. This is a primal necessity in a situation that will inevitably develop and on it will depend, more than on any other factor, the success of the social revolution. Industrial preparation is the most essential point, for without it the revolution is doomed to collapse.

The engineers and other technical specialists are more likely to join hands with labour when the social revolution comes, particularly if a closer bond and better understanding have in the meantime been established between the manual and mental workers.

Should they refuse and should the workers have failed to prepare themselves industrially and technically, then production would depend on *compelling* the willfully obstinate to co-operate – an experiment tried in the Russian Revolution and proved a complete failure.

The grave mistake of the Bolsheviks in this connection was their hostile treatment of the whole class of the intelligentsia on account of the opposition of some members of it. It was the spirit of intolerance, inherent in fanatical dogma, which caused them to persecute an entire social group because of the fault of a few. This manifested itself in the policy of wholesale vengeance upon the professional elements, the technical specialists, the cooperative organisations, and all cultured persons in general. Most of them, at first friendly to the Revolution, some even enthusiastic in its favour, were alienated by these Bolshevik tactics, and their cooperation was made impossible. As a result of their dictatorial attitude the communists were led to resort to increased oppression and tyranny till they finally introduced purely martial methods in the industrial life of the country. It was the era of compulsory labour, the militarisation of factory and mill, which unavoidably ended in disaster, because forced labour is, by the very nature of coercion, bad and inefficient; moreover, those so compelled react upon the situation by willful sabotage, by systematic delay and spoilage of work, which an intelligent enemy can practise in a way that cannot be detected in due time and which results in greater harm to machinery and product than direct refusal to work. In spite of the most drastic measures against this kind of sabotage, in spite even of the death penalty, the government was powerless to overcome the evil. The placing of a Bolshevik, of a political commissar, over every technician in the more responsible positions did not help matters. It merely created a legion of parasitic officials who, ignorant of industrial matters, only interfered with the work of those friendly to the Revolution and willing to aid, while their unfamiliarity with the task in no way prevented continued sabotage. The system of forced labour finally developed in what practically became economic counter-revolution, and no efforts of the dictatorship could alter the situation. It was this that caused the Bolsheviks to change from compulsory labour to a policy of winning over the specialists and technicians by returning them to authority in the industries and rewarding them with high pay and special emoluments.

It would be stupid and criminal to try again the methods which have so signally failed in the Russian Revolution and which, by their very character, are bound to fail every time, both industrially and morally.

The only solution of this problem is the already suggested preparation and training of the workers in the art of organising and managing industry, as well as closer contact between the manual and technical men. Every factory, mine, and mill should have its special workers' council, separate from and independent of the shop committee, for the purpose of familiarising the workers with the various phases of their particular industry, including the sources of raw material, the consecutive processes of manufacture, by-products, and manner of distribution. This industrial council should be permanent, but its membership must rotate in such a manner as to take in practically all the employees of a given factory or mill. To illustrate: suppose the industrial council in a certain establishment consists of five members or of twenty-five, as the case may be, according to the complexity of the industry and the size of the particular factory. The members of the council, after having thoroughly acquainted themselves with their industry, publish what they had learned for the information of their fellow-workers, and new council members are chosen to continue the industrial studies. In this manner the whole factory or mill can consecutively acquire the necessary knowledge about the organisation and management of their trade and keep step with its development. These councils would serve as industrial colleges where the workers would become familiar with the technique of their industry in all its phases.

At the same time the larger organisation, the union, must use every effort to compel capital to permit greater labour participation in the actual management. But this, even at best, can benefit only a small minority of the workers. The plan suggested above, on the other hand, opens the possibility of industrial training to practically every worker in shop, mill, and factory.

It is true, of course, that there are certain kinds of work – such as engineering: civil, electrical, mechanical – which the industrial councils will not be able to acquire by actual practice. But what they will learn of the general processes of industry will be of inestimable value as preparation. For the rest, the closer bond of friendship and cooperation between worker and technician is a paramount necessity.

The taking over of the industries is therefore the first great object of the social revolution. It is to be accomplished by the proletariat, by the part of it organised and prepared for the task. Considerable numbers of workers are already beginning to realise the importance of this and to understand the task before them. But understanding what is necessary to be done is not sufficient. Learning how to do it is the next step. It is up to the organised working class to enter at once upon this preparatory work.

Chapter 11

PRINCIPLES AND PRACTICE

The main purpose of the social revolution must be the *immediate* betterment of conditions for the masses. The success of the revolution fundamentally depends on it. This can be achieved only by organising consumption and production so as to be of real benefit to the populace. In that lies the greatest – in fact, the only – security of the social revolution. It was not the Red army which conquered counter-revolution in Russia: it was the peasants holding on for dear life to the land they had taken during the upheaval. The social revolution must be of material gain to the masses if it is to live and grow. The people at large must be sure of actual advantage from their efforts, or at least entertain the hope of such advantage in the near future. The revolution is doomed if it relies for its existence and defence on *mechanical* means, such as war and armies. The real safety of the revolution is *organic*; that is, it lies in industry and production.

The object of revolution is to secure greater freedom, to increase the material welfare of the people. The aim of the social revolution, in particular, is to enable the masses *by their own efforts* to bring about conditions of material and social well-being, to rise to higher moral and spiritual levels.

In other words, it is liberty which is to be established by the social revolution. For true liberty is based on economic opportunity. Without it all liberty is a sham and lie, a mask for exploitation and oppression. In the profoundest sense liberty is the daughter of economic equality.

The main aim of the social revolution is therefore to establish equal liberty on the basis of equal opportunity. The revolutionary re-organisation of life must immediately proceed to secure the equality of all, economically, politically, and socially.

That re-organisation will depend, first and foremost, on the thorough familiarity of labour with the economic situation of the country: on a complete inventory of the supply, on exact knowledge of the sources of raw material, and on the proper organisation of the labour forces for efficient management.

It means that statistics and intelligent workers' associations are vital needs of the revolution, on the day after the upheaval. The entire problem of production and distribution – the life of the revolution – is based on it. It is obvious, as pointed out before, that this knowledge must be acquired by the workers *before* the revolution if the latter is to accomplish its purposes.

That is why the shop and factory committee, dealt with in the previous chapter, are so important and will play such a decisive role in the revolutionary re-construction.

For a new society is not born suddenly, any more than a child is. New social life gestates in the body of the old just as new individual life does in the mother's womb. Time and certain processes are required to develop it till it becomes a complete organism capable of functioning. When that stage has been reached birth takes place in agony and pain, socially as individually. Revolution, to use a trite but expressive saying, is the midwife of the new social being. This is true in the most literal sense. Capitalism is the parent of the new society; the shop and factory committee, the union of class-conscious labour and revolutionary aims, is the germ of the new life. In that shop committee and union the worker must acquire the knowledge of how to manage his affairs: in the process he will grow to the perception that social life is a matter of proper organisation, of united effort, of solidarity. He will come to understand that it is not the bossing and ruling of men but free association and harmonious working together which accomplish things; that it is not government and laws which produce and create, make the wheat grow and the wheels turn, but concord and co-operation. Experience will teach him to substitute the management of things in place of the government of men. In the daily life and struggles of his shop committee the worker must learn how to conduct the revolution.

Shop and factory committees, organised locally, by district, region, and state, and federated nationally, will be the bodies best suited to carry on revolutionary production.

Local and State labour councils, federated nationally, will be the form of organisation most adapted to manage distribution by means of the people's co-operatives.

These committees, elected by the workers on the job, connect their shop and factory with other shops and factories of the same industry. The Joint Council of an entire industry links that industry with other industries, and thus is formed a federation of labour councils for the entire country.

Co-operative associations are the mediums of exchange between the country and city. The farmers, organised locally and federated regionally and nationally, supply the needs of the cities by means of the co-operatives and receive through the latter in exchange the products of the city industries.

Every revolution is accompanied by a great outburst of popular enthusiasm full of hope and aspiration. It is the spring-board of revolution. This high tide, spontaneous and powerful, opens up the human sources of initiative and activity. The sense of equality liberates the best there is in man and makes him consciously creative. These are the great motors of the social revolution, its moving forces. Their free and unhindered expression signifies the development and deepening of the revolution. Their suppression means decay and death. The revolution is safe, it grows and becomes strong, as long as the masses feel that they are direct participants in it, that they are fashioning their own lives, that they are making the revolution, that they *are* the revolution. But the moment their activities are usurped by a political party or are centred in some special organisation, revolutionary effort becomes limited to a comparatively small circle from which the large masses are practically excluded. The natural result is that popular enthusiasm is dampened, interest gradually weakens, initiative languishes, creativeness wanes, and the revolution becomes the monopoly of a clique which presently turns dictator.

This is fatal to the revolution. The sole prevention of such a catastrophe lies in the continued active interest of the workers through their everyday participation in all matters pertaining to the revolution. The source of this interest and activity is the shop and the union.

The interest of the masses and their loyalty to the revolution depend furthermore on their feeling that the revolution represents justice and fair play. This explains why revolutions have the power of rousing the people to acts of great heroism and devotion. As already pointed out, the masses instinctively see in revolution the enemy of wrong and iniquity and the harbinger of justice. In this sense revolution is a highly ethical factor and an inspiration. Fundamentally it is only great moral principles which can fire the masses and lift them to spiritual heights.

All popular upheavals have shown this to be true; particularly so the Russian Revolution. It was because of that spirit that the Russian masses so strikingly triumphed over all obstacles in the days of February and October. No opposition could conquer their devotion inspired by a great and noble cause. But the Revolution began to decline when it had become emasculated of its high moral values, when it was denuded of its elements of justice, equality, and liberty. Their loss was the doom of the Revolution.

It cannot be emphasised too strongly how essential spiritual values are to the social revolution. These and the consciousness of the masses that the revolution also means material betterment are dynamic influences in the life and growth of the new society. Of the two factors the spiritual values are foremost. The history of previous revolutions proves that the masses were ever willing to suffer and to sacrifice material well-being for the sake of greater liberty and justice. Thus in Russia neither cold nor starvation could induce the peasants and workers to aid counter-revolution. All privation and misery notwithstanding they served heroically the interests of the great cause. It was only when they saw the Revolution monopolised by a political party, the new-won liberties curtailed, a dictatorship established, and injustice and inequality dominant again that they became indifferent to the Revolution, declined to participate in the sham, refused to cooperate, and even turned against it.

To forget ethical values, to introduce practices and methods inconsistent with or opposed to the high moral purposes of the revolution means to invite counter-revolution and disaster.

It is therefore clear that the success of the social revolution primarily depends on liberty and equality. Any deviation from them can only be harmful; indeed, is sure to prove destructive. It follows that *all* the activities of the revolution must be based on freedom and equal rights. This applies to small things as to great. Any acts or methods tending to limit liberty, to create inequality and injustice, can result only in a popular attitude inimical to the revolution and in best interests.

It is from this angle that all the problems of the revolutionary period must be considered and solved. Among those problems the most important are consumption and housing, production and exchange.

Emma Goldman with Alexander Berkman in 1917

Chapter 12

CONSUMPTION AND EXCHANGE

Let us take up the organisation of consumption first, because people have to eat before they can work and produce.

"What do you mean by the organisation of consumption?" your friend asks.

"He means rationing, I suppose," you remark.

I do. Of course, when the social revolution has become thoroughly organised and production is functioning normally there will be enough for everybody. But in the first stages of the revolution, during the process of reconstruction, we must take care to supply the people as best we can, and equally, which means rationing.

"The Bolsheviks did not have equal rationing," your friend interrupts; "they had different kinds of rations for different people."

They did, and that was one of the greatest mistakes they made. It was resented by the people as a wrong and it provoked irritation and discontent. The Bolsheviks had one kind of ration for the sailor, another of lower quality and quantity for the soldier, a third for the skilled worker, a fourth for the unskilled one; another ration again for the average citizen, and yet another for the bourgeois. The best rations were for the Bolsheviks, the members of the Party, and special rations for the communist officials and commissars. At one time they had as many as fourteen different food rations. Your own common sense will tell you that it was all wrong. Was it fair to discriminate against people because they happened to be labourers, mechanics, or intellectuals rather than soldiers or sailors? Such methods were unjust and vicious: they immediately created material inequality and opened the door to misuse of position and opportunity, to speculation, graft, and swindle. They also stimulated counter-revolution, for those indifferent or unfriendly to the Revolution were embittered by the discrimination and therefore became an easy prey to counter-revolutionary influences.

This initial discrimination and the many others which followed were not dictated by the needs of the situation but solely by political party considerations. Having usurped the reins of government and fearing the opposition of the people, the Bolsheviks sought to strengthen themselves in the government seat by currying favour with the sailors, soldiers, and workers. But by these means they succeeded only in creating indignation and antagonising the masses, for the injustice of the system was too crying and obvious. Furthermore, even the 'favoured class', the proletariat, felt discriminated against because the soldiers were given better rations. Was the worker not as good as the soldier? Could the soldier fight for the Revolution – the factory man argued – if the worker would not supply him with ammunition? The soldier, in his turn, protested against the sailor getting more. Was he not as valuable as the sailor? And all condemned the special rations and privileges bestowed on the Bolshevik members of the Party, and particularly the comforts and even luxuries enjoyed by the higher officials and commissars, while the masses suffered privation.

Popular resentment of such practices was strikingly expressed by the Kronstadt sailors. It was in the midst of an extremely severe and hungry winter, in March 1921, that a public mass-meeting of the sailors unanimously resolved voluntarily to give up their extra rations on behalf of the less favoured population of Kronstadt, and to equalise the rations in the entire city. This truly ethical revolutionary action voiced the general feeling against discrimination and favouritism, and gave convincing proof of the deep sense of justice inherent in the masses.

All experience teaches that the just and square thing is at the same time also the most sensible and practical in the long run. This holds equally true of the individual as of collective life. Discrimination and injustice are particularly destructive to revolution, because the very spirit of revolution is born of the hunger for equity and justice.

I have already mentioned that when the social revolution attains the stage where it can produce sufficient for all, then is adopted the anarchist principle of 'to each according to his needs.' In the more industrially developed and efficient countries that stage would naturally be reached sooner than in backward lands. But until it is reached, the system of equal sharing, equal distribution per capita, is imperative as the only just method. It goes without saying, of course, that special consideration must be given to the sick and the old, to children, and to women during and after pregnancy, as was also the practice in the Russian Revolution.

"Let me get this straight," you remark. "There is to be equal sharing, you say. Then you won't be able to buy anything?"

No, there will be no buying or selling. The revolution abolishes private ownership of the means of production and distribution, and with it goes capitalistic business. Personal possession remains only in the things you use. Thus, your watch is your own, but the watch factory belongs to the people. Land, machinery, and all other public utilities will be collective property, neither to be bought nor sold. Actual use will be considered the only title – not to ownership but to possession. The organisation of the coal miners, for example, will be in charge of the coal mines, not as owners but as the operating agency. Similarly will the railroad brotherhoods run the railroads, and so on. Collective possession, co-operatively managed in the interests of the community, will take the place of personal ownership privately conducted for profit.

"But if you can't buy anything, then what's the use of money?" you ask.

None whatever; money becomes useless. You can't get anything for it. When the sources of supply, the land, factories, and products become public property, socialised, you can neither buy nor sell. As money is only a medium for such transactions, it loses its usefulness.

"But how will you exchange things?"

Exchange will be free. The coal miners, for instance, will deliver the coal they mined to the public coal yards for the use of the community. In their turn the miners will receive from the community's warehouses the machinery, tools, and the other commodities they need. That means free exchange without the medium of money and without profit, on the basis of requirement and the supply on hand.

"But if there is no machinery or food to be given to the miners?"

If there is none, money will not help matters. The miners couldn't feed on banknotes. Consider how such things are managed today. You trade coal for money, and for the money you get food. The free community we are speaking of will exchange the coal for food directly, without the medium of money.

"But on what basis? Today you know what a dollar is worth, more or less, but how much coal will you give for a sack of flour?"

You mean, how will value or price be determined. But we have seen already in preceding chapters that there is no real measure of value, and that price depends on supply and demand and varies accordingly. The price of coal rises if there is a scarcity of it; it becomes cheaper if the supply is greater than the demand. To make bigger profits the coal owners artificially limit the output, and the same methods obtain throughout the capitalistic system. With the abolition of capitalism no one will be interested in raising the price of coal or limiting its supply. As much coal will be mined as will be necessary to satisfy the need. Similarly will as much food be raised as the country needs. It will be the *requirements* of the community and the supply obtainable which will determine the amount it is to receive. This applies to coal and food as to all other needs of the people.

"But suppose there is not enough of a certain product to go around. What will you do then?"

Then we'll do what is done even in capitalistic society in time of war and scarcity: the people are rationed, with the difference that in the free community rationing will be managed on principles of equality.

"But suppose the farmer refuses to supply the city with his products unless he gets money?"

The farmer, like any one else, wants money only if he can buy with it the things he needs. He will quickly see that money is useless to him. In Russia during the Revolution you could not get a peasant to sell you a pound of flour for a bagful of money. But he was eager to give you a barrel of the finest grain for an old pair of boots. It is ploughs, spades, rakes, agricultural machinery, and clothing which the farmer wants, not money. For these he will let you have his wheat, barley, and corn. In other words, the city will exchange with the farm the products each requires, on the basis of need.

It has been suggested by some that exchange during the re-construction should be based on some definite standard. It is proposed, for example, that every community issue its own money, as is often done in time of revolution; or that a day's work should be considered the unit of value and so-called labour notes serve as medium of exchange. But neither of these proposals is of practical help. Money issued by communities in revolution would quickly depreciate to the point of no value, since such money would have no secure guarantees behind it, without which money is worth nothing. Similarly labour notes would not represent any definite and measurable value as a means of exchange. What would, for instance, an hour's work of the coal miner be worth? Or fifteen minutes' consultation with the physician? Even if all effort should be considered equal in value and an hour's labour be made the unit, could the house painter's hour of work or the surgeon's operation be equitably measured in terms of wheat?

Common sense will solve this problem on the basis of human equality and the right of every one to life.

"Such a system might work among decent people," your friend objects; "but how about shirkers? Were not the Bolsheviks right in establishing the principle that 'whoever doesn't work, doesn't eat'?"

No, my friend, you are mistaken. At first sight it may appear as if that was a just and sensible idea. But in reality it proved impractical, not to speak of the injustice and harm it worked all around.

"How so?"

It was impractical because it required an army of officials to keep tabs on the people who worked or didn't work. It led to incrimination and recrimination and endless disputes about official decisions. So that within a short time the number of those who didn't work was doubled and even trebled by the effort to force people to work and to guard against their dodging or doing bad work. It was the system of compulsory labour which soon proved such a failure that the Bolsheviks were compelled to give it up.

Moreover, the system caused even greater evils in other directions. Its injustice lay in the fact that you cannot break into a person's heart or mind and decide what peculiar physical or mental condition makes it temporarily impossible for him to work. Consider further the precedent you establish by introducing a false principle and thereby rousing the opposition of those who feel it wrong and oppressive and therefore refuse co-operation.

A rational community will find it more practical and beneficial to treat all alike, whether one happens to work at the time or not, rather than create more non-workers to watch those already on hand, or to build prisons for their punishment and support. For if you refuse to feed a man, for whatever cause, you drive him to theft and other crimes – and thus you yourself create the necessity for courts, lawyers, judges, jails, and warders, the upkeep of whom is far more burdensome than to feed the offenders. And these you have to feed, anyhow, even if you put them in prison.

The revolutionary community will depend more on awakening the social consciousness and solidarity of its delinquents than on punishment. It will rely on the example set by its working members, and it will be right in doing so. For the natural attitude of the industrious man to the shirker is such that the latter will find the social atmosphere so unpleasant that he will prefer to work and enjoy the respect and good will of his fellows rather than to be despised in idleness.

Bear in mind that it is more important, and in the end more practical and useful, to do the square thing rather than to gain a seeming immediate advantage. That is, to do justice is more vital than to punish. For punishment is never just and always harmful to both sides, the punished and the punisher, harmful even more spiritually than physically, and there is no greater harm than that, for it hardens and corrupts you. This is unqualifiedly true of your individual life and with the same force it applies to the collective social existence.

On the foundations of liberty, justice, and equality, as also on understanding and sympathy, must be built every phase of life in the social revolution. Only so it can endure. This applies to the problems of shelter, food, and the security of your district or city, as well as to the defence of the revolution.

As regards housing and local safety Russia has shown the way in the first months of the October Revolution. House committees, chosen by the tenants, and city federations of such committees, take the problem in hand. They gather statistics of the facilities of a given district and of the number of applicants requiring quarters. The latter are assigned according to personal or family need on the basis of equal rights.

Similar house and district committees have charge of the provisioning of the city. Individual application for rations at the distributing centres is a stupendous waste of time and energy. Equally false is the system, practiced in Russia in the first years of the Revolution, of issuing rations in the institutions of one's employment, in shops, factories, and offices. The better and more efficient way, which at the same time insures more equitable distribution and closes the door to favouritism and misuse, is rationing by houses or streets. The authorised house or street committee procures at the local distributing centre the provisions, clothing, etc., apportioned to the number of tenants represented by the committee. Equal rationing has the added advantage of eradicating food speculation, the vicious practice which grew to enormous proportions in Russia because of the system of inequality and privilege. Party members or persons with a political pull could freely bring to the cities car-loads of flour while some old peasant woman was severely punished for selling a loaf of bread. No wonder speculation flourished, and to such an extent, indeed, that the Bolsheviks had to form special regiments to cope with the evil. The prisons were filled with offenders; capital punishment was resorted to; but even the most drastic measures of the government failed to stop speculation, for the latter was the direct consequence of the system of discrimination and favouritism. Only equality and freedom of exchange can obviate such evils or at least reduce them to a minimum.

Taking care of the sanitary and kindred needs of street and district by voluntary committees of house and locality affords the best results, since such bodies, themselves tenants of the given district, are personally interested in the health and safety of their families and friends. This system worked much better in Russia than the subsequently established regular police force. The latter consisting mostly of the worst city elements, proved corrupt, brutal, and oppressive.

The hope of material betterment is, as already mentioned, a powerful factor in the forward movement of humanity. But that incentive alone is not sufficient to inspire the masses to give them the vision of a new and better world, and cause them to face danger and privation for its sake. For that an ideal is needed, an ideal which appeals not only to the stomach but even more to the heart and imagination, which rouses our dormant longing for what is fine and beautiful, for the spiritual and cultural values of life. An ideal, in short, which wakens the inherent social instincts of man, feeds his sympathies and fellow-feeling, fires his love of liberty and justice, and imbues even the lowest with nobility of thought and deed, as we frequently witness in the catastrophic events of life. Let a great tragedy happen anywhere – an earthquake, flood, or railroad accident – and the compassion of the whole world goes out to the sufferers. Acts of heroic self-sacrifice, of brave rescue, and of unstinted aid demonstrate the real nature of man and his deep-felt brotherhood and unity.

This is true of mankind in all times, climes, and social strata. The story of Amundsen is a striking illustration of it. After decades of arduous and dangerous work the famous Norwegian explorer resolves to enjoy his remaining years in peaceful literary pursuits. He is announcing his decision at a banquet given in his honour, and almost at the same moment comes the news that the Nobile expedition to the North Pole had met with disaster. On the instant Amundsen renounces all his plans of a quiet life and prepares to fly to the aid of the lost aviators, fully aware of the peril of such an undertaking. Human sympathy and the compelling impulse to help those in distress overcome all considerations of personal safety, and Amundsen sacrifices his life in an attempt to rescue the Nobile party.

Deep in all of us lives the spirit of Amundsen. How many men of science have given up their lives in seeking knowledge by which to benefit their fellow-men – how many physicians and nurses have perished in the work of ministering to people stricken with contagious disease – how many men and women have voluntarily faced certain death in the effort to check an epidemic which was decimating their country or even some foreign land – how many men, common working men, miners, sailors, railroad employees – unknown to fame and unsung – have given themselves in the spirit of Amundsen? Their name is legion.

It is *this* human nature, this idealism, which must be roused by the social revolution. Without it the revolution cannot be, without it, it cannot live. Without it man is forever doomed to remain a slave and a weakling.

It is the work of the anarchist, of the revolutionist, of the intelligent, class-conscious proletarian to exemplify and cultivate this spirit and instil it in others. It alone can conquer the powers of evil and darkness, and build a new world of humanity, liberty, and justice.

Nestor Makhno and Alexander Berkman in Paris, around 1927

Chapter 13

PRODUCTION

"What about production?" you ask; "how is it to be managed?"

We have already seen what principles must underlie the activities of the revolution if it is to be social and accomplish its aims. The same principles of freedom and voluntary co-operation must also direct the re-organisation of the industries.

The first effect of the revolution is reduced production. The general strike, which I have forecast as the starting point of the social revolution, itself constitutes a suspension of industry. The workers lay down their tools, demonstrate in the streets, and thus temporarily stop production.

But life goes on. The essential needs of the people must be satisfied. In that stage the revolution lives on the supplies, already on hand. But to exhaust those supplies would be disastrous. The situation rests in the hands of labour: the immediate resumption of industry is imperative. The organised agricultural and industrial proletariat takes possession of the land, factories, shops, mines and mills. Most energetic application is now the order of the day.

It should be clearly understood that the *social revolution necessitates more intensive production* than under capitalism in order to supply the needs of the large masses who till then had lived in penury. This greater production can be achieved only by the workers having previously prepared themselves for the new situation. Familiarity with the processes of industry, knowledge of the sources of supply, and determination to succeed will accomplish the task. The enthusiasm generated by the revolution, the energies liberated, and the inventiveness stimulated by it must be given full freedom and scope to find creative channels. Revolution always wakens a high degree of responsibility. Together with the new atmosphere of liberty and brotherhood it creates the realisation that hard work and severe self-discipline are necessary to bring production up to the requirements of consumption.

On the other hand, the new situation will greatly simplify the present very complex problems of industry. For you must consider that capitalism, because of its competitive character and contradictory financial and commercial interests, involves many intricate and perplexing issues which would be entirely eliminated by the abolition of the conditions of today. Questions of wage scales and selling prices; the requirements of the existing markets and the hunt for new ones; the scarcity of capital for large operations and the heavy interest to be paid on it; new investments, the effects of speculation and monopoly, and a score of related problems which worry the capitalist and make industry such a difficult and cumbersome network today would all disappear. At present these require divers departments of study and highly trained men to keep unraveling the tangled skein of plutocratic cross purposes, many specialists to calculate the actualities and possibilities of profit and loss, and a large force of aids to help steer the industrial ship between the perilous rocks which beset the chaotic course of capitalist competition, national and international.

All this would be automatically done away with by the socialisation of industry and the termination of the competitive system; and thereby the problems of production will be immensely lightened. The knotted complexity of capitalist industry need therefore inspire no undue fear for the future. Those who talk of labour not being equal to manage 'modern' industry fail to take into account the factors referred to above. The industrial labyrinth will turn out to be far less formidable on the day of the social reconstruction.

In passing it may be mentioned that all the other phases of life would also be very much simplified as a result of the indicated changes: various present-day habits, customs, compulsory and unwholesome modes of living will naturally fall into disuse.

Furthermore it must be considered that the task of increased production would be enormously facilitated by the addition to the ranks of labour of vast numbers whom the altered economic conditions will liberate for work.

Recent statistics show that in 1920 there were in the United States over 41 million persons of both sexes engaged in gainful occupations out of a total population of over 105 millions. Out of those 41 millions only 26 millions were actually employed in the industries, including transportation and agriculture, the balance of 15 millions consisting mostly of persons engaged in trade, of commercial travellers, advertisers, and various other middlemen of the present system. In other words, 15 million persons would be released for useful work by a revolution in the United States. A similar situation, proportionate to population, would develop in other countries.

The greater production necessitated by the social revolution would therefore have an additional army of many million persons at its disposal. The systematic incorporation of those millions into industry and agriculture, aided by modern scientific methods of organisation and production, will go a long way toward helping to solve the problems of supply.

Capitalist production is for profit; more labour is used today to sell things than to produce them. The social revolution re-organises the industries on the basis of the *needs* of the populace. Essential needs come first, naturally. Food, clothing, shelter – these are the primal requirements of man. The first step in this direction is the ascertaining of the available supply of provisions and other commodities. The labour associations in every city and community take this work in hand for the purpose of equitable distribution. Workers' committees in every street and district assume charge, co-operating with similar committees in the city and state, and federating their efforts throughout the country by means of general councils of producers and consumers.

Great events and upheavals bring to the fore the most active and energetic elements. The social revolution will crystallise the class-conscious labour ranks. By whatever name they will be known – as industrial unions, revolutionary syndicalist bodies, co-operative associations, leagues of producers and consumers – they will represent the most enlightened and advanced part of labour, the organised workers aware of their aims and how to attain them. It is they who will be the moving spirit of the revolution.

With the aid of industrial machinery and by scientific cultivation of the land freed from monopoly, the revolution must first of all supply the elemental wants of society. In farming and gardening, intensive cultivation and modern methods have made us practically independent of natural soil quality and climate. To a very considerable extent man now makes his own soil and his own climate, thanks to the achievements of chemistry. Exotic fruits can be raised in the north to be supplied to the warm south, as is being done in France. Science is the wizard who enables man to master all difficulties and overcome all obstacles. The future, liberated from the incubus of the profit system and enriched by the work of the millions of non-producers of today, holds the greatest welfare for society. That future must be the objective point of the social revolution; its motto: bread and well-being for all. First bread, then well-being and luxury. Even luxury, for luxury is a deep-felt need of man, a need of his physical as of his spiritual being.

Intense application to this purpose must be the continuous effort of the revolution: not something to be postponed for a distant day but of immediate practice. The revolution must strive to enable every community to sustain itself, to become materially independent. No country should have to rely on outside help or exploit colonies for its support. That is the way of capitalism. The aim of anarchism, on the contrary, is material independence, not only for the individual, but for every community.

This means gradual decentralisation instead of centralisation. Even under capitalism we see the decentralisation tendency manifest itself in spite of the essentially centralistic character of the present-day industrial system. Countries which were before entirely dependent on foreign manufactures, as Germany in the last quarter of the nineteenth century, later Italy and Japan, and now Hungary, Czechoslovakia, etc., are gradually emancipating themselves industrially, working their own natural resources, building their own factories and mills, and attaining economic independence from other lands. International finance does not welcome this development and tries its utmost to retard its progress, because it is more profitable for the Morgans and Rockefellers to keep such countries as Mexico, China, India, Ireland, or Egypt industrially backward, in order to exploit their natural resources and at the same time be assured of foreign markets for 'over-production' at home. The governments of the great financiers and lords of industry help them secure those foreign natural resources and markets, even at the point of the bayonet. Thus Great Britain by force of arms compels China to permit English opium to poison the Chinese, at a good profit, and exploits every means to dispose in that country of the greater part of its textile products. For the same reason Egypt, India, Ireland, and other dependencies and colonies are not permitted to develop their home industries.

In short, capitalism seeks centralisation. But a free country needs decentralisation, independence not only political but also industrial and economic.

Russia strikingly illustrates how imperative economic independence is, particularly to the social revolution. For years following the October upheaval the Bolshevik Government concentrated its efforts on currying favour with bourgeois governments for 'recognition' and inviting foreign capitalists to help exploit the resources of Russia. But capital, afraid to make large investments under the insecure conditions of the dictatorship, failed to respond with any degree of enthusiasm. Meanwhile Russia was approaching economic breakdown. The situation finally compelled the Bolsheviks to understand that the country must depend on her own efforts for maintenance. Russia began to look around for means to help herself; and thereby she acquired greater confidence in her own abilities, learned to exercise self-reliance and initiative, and started to develop her own industries; a slow and painful process, but a wholesome necessity which will ultimately make Russia economically self-supporting and independent.

The social revolution in any given country must from the very first determine to make itself self-supporting. *It must help itself.* This principle of self-help is not to be understood as a lack of solidarity with other lands. On the contrary, mutual aid and co-operation between countries, as among individuals, can exist only on the basis of equality, among equals. *Dependence* is the very reverse of it.

Should the social revolution take place in several countries at the same time – in France and Germany, for instance – then joint effort would be a matter of course and would make the task of revolutionary re-organisation much easier.

Fortunately the workers are learning to understand that their cause is international: the organisation of labour is now developing beyond national boundaries. It is to be hoped that the time is not far away when the entire proletariat of Europe may combine in a general strike, which is to be the prelude to the social revolution. That is emphatically a consummation to have striven for with the greatest earnestness. But at the same time the probability is not to be discounted that the revolution may break out in one country sooner than in another – let us say in France earlier than in Germany – and in such a case it would become imperative for France not to wait for possible aid from outside but immediately to exert all her energies to help herself, to supply the most essential needs of her people by her own efforts.

Every country in revolution must seek to achieve agricultural independence no less than political, industrial self-help no less than agricultural. This process is going on to a certain extent even under capitalism. It should be one of the main objects of the social revolution. Modern methods make it possible. The manufacture of watches and clocks, for example, which was formerly a monopoly of Switzerland, is now carried on in every country. Production of silk, previously limited to France, is among the great industries of various countries today. Italy, without sources of coal or iron, constructs steel-clad ships. Switzerland, no richer, also makes them.

Decentralisation will cure society of many evils of the centralised principle. Politically decentralisation means freedom; industrially, material independence; socially it implies security and well-being for the small communities; individually it results in manhood and liberty.

Equally important to the social revolution as independence from foreign lands is decentralisation within the country itself. Internal decentralisation means making the larger regions, even every community, so far as possible, self-supporting. In his very illuminating and suggestive work, *Fields, Factories, and Workshops*, Peter Kropotkin has convincingly shown how a city like Paris even, now almost exclusively commercial, could raise enough food in its own environs to support its population abundantly. By using modern agricultural machinery and intensive cultivation London and New York could subsist upon the products raised in their own immediate vicinity. It is a fact that "our means of obtaining from the soil whatever we want, under *any* climate and upon *any* soil, have lately been improved at such a rate that we cannot foresee yet what is the limit of productivity of a few acres of land. The limit vanishes in proportion to our better study of the subject, and every year makes it vanish further and further from our sight."

When the social revolution begins in any land, its foreign commerce stops: the importation of raw materials and finished products is suspended. The country may even be blockaded by the bourgeois governments, as was the case with Russia. Thus the revolution is *compelled* to become self-supporting and provide for its own wants. Even various parts of the same country may have to face such an eventuality. They would have to produce what they need within their own area, by their own efforts. Only decentralisation could solve this problem. The country would have to re-organise its activities in such a manner as to be able to feed itself. It would have to revert to production on a small scale, to home industry, and to intensive agriculture and horticulture. Man's initiative freed by the revolution and his wits sharpened by necessity will rise to the situation.

It must therefore be clearly understood that it would be disastrous to the interests of the revolution to suppress or interfere with the small-scale industries which are even now practiced to such a great extent in various European countries. Numerous articles of everyday use are produced by the peasants of Continental Europe during their leisure winter hours. Those home manufactures total up tremendous figures and fill a great need. It would be most harmful to the revolution to destroy them, as Russia so foolishly did in her mad Bolshevik passion for centralisation. When a country in revolution is attacked by foreign governments, when it is blockaded and deprived of imports, when its large-scale industries threaten to break down or the railroads actually do break down, then it is just the small home industries which become the vital nerve of economic life: they alone can feed and save the revolution.

Moreover, such home industries are not only a potent economic factor; they are also of the greatest social value. They serve to cultivate friendly intercourse between the farm and the city, bringing the two into closer and more solidaric contact. In face, the home industries are themselves an expression of a most wholesome social spirit which from earliest times has manifested itself in village gatherings, in communal efforts, in folk dance and song. This normal and healthy tendency, in its various aspects, should be encouraged and stimulated by the revolution for the greater weal of the community.

The role of industrial decentralisation in the revolution is unfortunately too little appreciated. Even in progressive labour ranks there is a dangerous tendency to ignore or minimise its importance. Most people are still in the thraldom of the Marxian dogma that centralisation is "more efficient and economical." They close their eyes to the fact that the alleged 'economy' is achieved at the cost of the worker's limb and life, that the 'efficiency' degrades him to a mere industrial cog, deadens his soul, and kills his body. Furthermore, in a system of centralisation the administration of industry becomes constantly merged in fewer hands, producing a powerful bureaucracy of industrial overlords. It would indeed be the sheerest irony if the revolution were to aim at such a result. It would mean the creation of a new master class.

The revolution can accomplish the emancipation of labour only by gradual decentralisation, by developing the individual worker into a more conscious and determining factor in the processes of industry, by making him the impulse whence proceeds all industrial and social activity. The deep significance of the social revolution lies in the abolition of the mastery of man over man, putting in its place the management of things. Only thus can be achieved industrial and social freedom.

"Are you sure it would work?" you demand.

I am sure of this: if that will not work, nothing else will. The plan I have outlined is a free communism, a life of voluntary co-operation and equal sharing. There is no other way of securing economic equality which alone is liberty. Any other system must lead back to capitalism.

It is likely, of course, that a country in social revolution may try various economic experiments. A limited capitalism might be introduced in one part of the land or collectivism in another. But collectivism is only another form of the wage system and it would speedily tend to become the capitalism of the present day. For collectivism begins by abolishing private ownership of the means of production and immediately reverses itself by returning to the system of remuneration according to work performed; which means the re-introduction of inequality.

Man learns by doing. The social revolution in different countries and regions will probably try out various methods, and by practical experience learn the best way. The revolution is at the same time the opportunity and justification for it. I am not attempting to prophesy what this or that country is going to do, what particular course it will follow. Nor do I presume to dictate to the future, to prescribe its mode of conduct. My purpose is to suggest, in broad outline, the principles which must animate the revolution, the general lines of action it should follow if it is to accomplish its aim – the reconstruction of society on a foundation of freedom and equality.

We know that previous revolutions for the most part failed of their objects; they degenerated into dictatorship and despotism, and thus re-established the old institutions of oppression and exploitation.

We know it from past and recent history. We therefore draw the conclusion that the old way will not do. A new way must be tried in the coming social revolution. What new way. The only one so far known to man: the way of liberty and equality, the way of free communism, of anarchy.

Chapter 14

DEFENCE OF THE REVOLUTION

"Suppose your system is tried, would you have any means of defending the revolution?" you ask.

Certainly.

"Even by armed force?"

Yes, if necessary.

"But armed force is organised violence. Didn't you say anarchism was against it?"

Anarchism is opposed to any interference with your liberty, be it by force and violence or by any other means. It is against all invasion and compulsion. But if any one attacks *you*, then it is *he* who is invading you, he who is employing violence against you. You have a right to defend yourself. More than that, it is your duty, as an anarchist, to protect your liberty, to resist coercion and compulsion. Otherwise you are a slave, not a free man. In other words, the social revolution will attack no one, but it will defend itself against invasion from any quarter.

Besides, you must not confuse the social revolution with anarchy. Revolution, in some of its stages, is a violent upheaval; anarchy is a social condition of freedom and peace. The revolution is the *means* of bringing anarchy about but it is not anarchy itself. It is to pave the road for anarchy, to establish conditions which will make a life of liberty possible.

But to achieve its purpose the revolution must be imbued with and directed by the anarchist spirit and ideas. The end shapes the means, just as the tool you use must be fit to do the work you want to accomplish. That is to say, the social revolution must be anarchistic in method as in aim.

Revolutionary defence muse be in consonance with this spirit. Self-defence excludes all acts of coercion, of persecution or revenge. It is concerned only with repelling attack and depriving the enemy of opportunity to invade you.

"How would you repel foreign invasion?"

By the strength of the revolution. In what does that strength consist? First and foremost, in the support of the people, in the devotion of the industrial and agricultural masses. If they feel that they themselves are making the revolution, that they have become the masters of their lives, that they have gained freedom and are building up their welfare, then in that very sentiment you have the greatest strength of the revolution. The masses fight today for king, capitalist, or president because they believe them worth fighting for. Let them believe in the revolution, and they will defend it to the death.

They will fight for the revolution with heart and soul, as the half-starved working men, women, and even children of Petrograd defended their city, almost with bare hands, against the White army of General Yudenitch. Take that faith away, deprive the people of power by setting up some authority over them, be it a political party or military organisation, and you have dealt a fatal blow to the revolution. You will have robbed it of its main source of strength, the masses. You will have made it defenceless.

The armed workers and peasants are the only effective defence of the revolution. By means of their unions and syndicates they must always be on guard against counter-revolutionary attack. The worker in factory and mill, in mine and field, is the soldier of the revolution. He is at his bench and plow or on the battlefield, according to need. But in his factory as in his regiment he is the soul of the revolution, and it is *his* will that decides its fate. In industry the shop committees, in the barracks the soldiers' committees – these are the fountain-head of all revolutionary strength and activity.

It was the volunteer Red Guard, made up of Boilers, that successfully defended the Russian Revolution in its most critical initial stages. Later on it was again volunteer peasant regiments who defeated the White armies. The regular Red army, organised later, was powerless without the volunteer workers' and peasants' divisions. Siberia was freed from Kolchak and his hordes by such peasant volunteers. In the north of Russia it was also workers' and peasants' detachments that drove out the foreign armies which came to impose the yoke of native reactionaries upon the people. In the Ukraine the volunteer peasant armies – known as *povstantsi* – saved the Revolution from numerous counter-revolutionary generals and particularly from Denikin when the latter was already at the very gates of Moscow. It was the revolutionary *povstantsi* who freed southern Russia from the invading armies of Germany, France, Italy, and Greece and subsequently also routed the White forces of General Wrangel.

The military defence of the revolution may demand a supreme command, co-ordination of activities, discipline, and obedience to orders. But these must proceed from the devotion of the workers and peasants, and must be based on their voluntary co-operation through their own local, regional, and federal organisations. In the matter of defence against foreign attack, as in all other problems of the social revolution, the active interest of the masses, their autonomy and self-determination are the best guarantee of success.

Understand well that the only really effective defence of the revolution lies in the attitude of the people. Popular discontent is the worst enemy of the revolution and its greatest danger. We must always bear in mind that the strength of the social revolution is organic, not mechanistic: not in mechanical, military measures lies its might, but industry, in its ability to reconstruct life, to establish liberty and justice. Let the people feel that it is indeed their own cause which is at stake, and the last man of them will fight like a lion on its behalf.

The same applies to internal as to external defence. What chance would any White general or counter-revolutionist have if he could not exploit oppression and injustice to incite the people against the revolution?

Counter-revolution can feed only on popular discontent. Where the masses are conscious that the revolution and all its activities are in their own hands, thee they themselves are managing things and are free to change their methods when they consider it necessary, counter-revolution can find no support and is harmless.

"But would you let counter-revolutionists incite the people if they tried to?"

By all means. Let them talk all they like. To restrain them would serve only to create a persecuted class and thereby enlist popular sympathy for them and their cause. To suppress speech and press is not only a theoretic offense against liberty: it is a direct blow at the very foundations of the revolution. It would, first of all, raise problems where none had existed before. It would introduce methods which must lead to discontent and opposition, to bitterness and strife, to prison, *Cheka* and civil war. It would generate fear and distrust, would hatch conspiracies, and culminate in a reign of terror which has always killed revolutions in the past.

The social revolution must from the very start be based on entirely different principles, on a new conception and attitude. Full freedom is the very breath of its existence; and be it never forgotten that the cure for evil and disorder is more liberty, not suppression. Suppression leads only to violence and destruction.

"Will you not defend the revolution then?" your friend demands.

Certainly we will. But not against mere talk, not against an expression of opinion. The revolution must be big enough to welcome even the severest criticism, and profit by it if it is justified. The revolution will defend itself most determinedly against real counter-revolution, against all active enemies, against any attempt to defeat or sabotage it by forcible invasion or violence. That is the right of the revolution and its duty. But it will not persecute the conquered foe, nor wreak vengeance upon an entire social class because of the fault of individual members of it. The sins of the fathers shall not be visited upon their children.

"What will you do with counter-revolutionists?"

Actual combat and armed resistance involve human sacrifices, and the counter-revolutionists who lose their lives under such circumstances suffer the unavoidable consequences of their deeds. But the revolutionary people are not savages. The wounded are not slaughtered nor those taken prisoners executed. Neither is practiced the barbarous system of shooting hostages, as the Bolsheviks did.

"How will you treat counter-revolutionists taken prisoners during an engagement?"

The revolution must find new ways, some sensible method of dealing with them. The old method is to imprison them, support them in idleness, and employ numerous men to guard and punish them. And while the culprit remains in prison, incarceration and brutal treatment still further embitter him against the revolution, strengthen his opposition, and nurse thoughts of vengeance and new conspiracies. The revolution will regard such methods as stupid and detrimental to its best interests. It will try instead by humane treatment to convince the defeated enemy of the error and uselessness of his resistance. It will apply liberty instead of revenge. It will take into consideration that most of the counter-revolutionists are dupes rather than enemies, deluded victims of some individuals seeking power and authority. It will know that they need enlightenment rather than punishment, and that the former will accomplish more than the latter. Even today this perception is gaining ground. The Bolsheviks defeated the Allied armies in Russia more effectively by revolutionary propaganda among the enemy soldiers than by the strength of their artillery. These new methods have been recognised as practical even by the United States Government which is making use of them now in its Nicaraguan campaign. American aeroplanes scatter proclamations and appeals to the Nicaraguan people to persuade them to desert Sandino and his cause, and the American army chiefs expect the best results from these tactics. But the Sandino patriots are fighting for home and country against a foreign invader, while counter-revolutionists wage war against their own people. The work of their enlightenment is much simpler and promises better results.

"Do you think that would really be the best way to deal with counter-revolution?"

By all means. Humane treatment and kindness are more effective than cruelty and vengeance. The new attitude in this regard would suggest also a number of other methods of similar character. Various modes of dealing with conspirators and active enemies of the revolution would develop as soon as you begin to practise the new policy. The plan might be adopted, for instance, of scattering them, individually or in small groups, over districts removed from their counter-revolutionary influences, among communities of revolutionary spirit and consciousness. Consider also that counter-revolutionists must eat; which means that they would find themselves in a situation that would claim their thoughts and time for other things than the hatching of conspiracies. The defeated counter-revolutionist, left at liberty instead of being imprisoned, would have to seek means of existence. He would not be denied his livelihood, of course, since the revolution would be generous enough to feed even its enemies. But the man in question would have to join some community, secure lodgings, and so forth, in order to enjoy the hospitality of the distributing centre. In other words, the counter-revolutionary 'prisoners in freedom' would depend on the community and the good will of its members for their means of existence. They would live in its atmosphere and be influenced by its revolutionary environment. Surely they will be safer and more contented than in prison, and presently they would cease to be a danger to the revolution. We have repeatedly seen such examples in Russia, in cases where counter-revolutionists had escaped the *Cheka* and settled down in some village or city, where as a result of considerate and decent treatment they became useful members of the community, often more zealous on behalf of the public welfare than the average citizen, while hundreds of their fellow-conspirators, who had not been lucky enough to avoid arrest, were busy in prison with thoughts of revenge and new plots.

Various plans of treating such 'prisoners in freedom' will no doubt be tried by the revolutionary people. But whatever the methods, they will be more satisfactory than the present system of revenge and punishment, the complete failure of which has been demonstrated throughout human experience. Among the new ways might also be tried that of free colonisation. The revolution will offer its enemies an opportunity to settle in some part of the country and there establish the form of social life that will suit them best. It is no vain speculation to foresee that it would not be long before most of them would prefer the brotherhood and liberty of the revolutionary community to the reactionary regime of their colony. But even if they did not, nothing would be lost. On the contrary, the revolution would itself be the greatest gainer, spiritually, by forsaking methods of revenge and persecution and practicing humanity and magnanimity. Revolutionary self-defence, inspired by such methods, will be the more effective because of the very freedom it will guarantee even to its enemies. Its appeal to the masses and to the world at large will thereby be the more irresistible and universal. In its justice and humanity lies the invincible strength of the social revolution.

No revolution has yet tried the true way of liberty. None has had sufficient faith in it. Force and suppression, persecution, revenge, and terror have characterised all revolutions in the past and have thereby defeated their original aims. The time has come to try new methods, new ways. The social revolution is to achieve the emancipation of man through liberty, but if we have no faith in the latter, revolution becomes a denial and betrayal of itself. Let us then have the courage of freedom: let it replace suppression and terror. Let liberty become our faith and our deed and we shall grow strong therein.

Only liberty can make the social revolution effective and wholesome. It alone can pave the way to greater heights and prepare a society where well-being and joy shall be the heritage of all. The day will dawn when man shall for the first time have full opportunity to grow and expand in the free and generous sunshine of anarchy.

ZAPATA OF MEXICO
by Peter E. Newell

Zapata was the leading figure of the Mexican Revolution of 1910 who fought for the rights of local communities against greedy landlords, treacherous politicians and foreign-owned companies. Under the slogan 'Land and Liberty!' he became the purest embodiment of the Mexican Revolution. Zapata's memory lives on in Mexico, and today's Zapatistas (the EZLN) take their inspiration from his life and struggle.

£9.50 (including postage and packing)   ISBN 1 904491 05 7

HISTORY OF THE MAKHNOVIST MOVEMENT 1918-21
by Peter Arshinov

During the Russian Revolution the old order was totally swept away, but in the midst of this the Bolsheviks were developing their own repression, far more brutal and totalitarian than what it replaced. Makhno's struggle to destroy both the old and the new oppressors is as significant today as it was then, and this is undoubtedly the most important source work available.

£9.90 (including postage and packing)   ISBN 1 900384 40 9

ANARCHISTS IN THE SPANISH REVOLUTION
by José Peirats

The most comprehensive critical history of the Spanish Civil War and the role played by the CNT-FAI, the anarcho-syndicalists and anarchists. The first part of this 388-page book also contains a brief survey of the working class movements in Spain going back to the foundation of the Spanish section of the First International in 1869 and the political struggles which were a prelude to the Civil War.

£12.50 (including postage and packing)   ISBN 0 900384 53 0

Available from Freedom Press, 84b Whitechapel High Street, London E1 7QX (payment with order please) or via our website at www.freedompress.org.uk

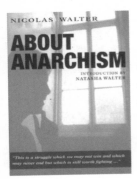

ABOUT ANARCHISM
by Nicolas Walter
introduction by Natasha Walter

This is a new edition of the classic work by Nicolas Walter, who was a writer, journalist and active protester against the power of the state. It has often been reprinted and been translated into many languages, including French, Spanish, Japanese, Serbo-Croat, Chinese, Polish and Russian. It includes a new introduction by Natasha Walter.

£4.20 (including postage and packing)   ISBN 0 900384 90 5

ANARCHY IN ACTION
by Colin Ward

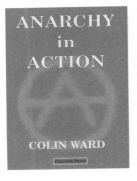

This book is not intended for people who have spent a lifetime pondering the problems of anarchism, but for those who either had no idea of what the word implied or knew exactly what it implied and rejected it, considering that it had no relevance for the modern world. It is about the many ways in which people organise themselves in any kind of human society ...

£5.95 (including postage and packing)   ISBN 0 900384 20 4

WHAT IS ANARCHISM?
An Introduction

Today the word anarchism inspires both fear and fascination, but few people seem to understand what anarchists believe, what anarchists want and what anarchists do. To help answer these questions are contributions from Michael Bakunin, Alexander Berkman, William Godwin, Peter Kropotkin, Errico Malatesta, William Morris, Rudolf Rocker, Donald Rooum, Philip Sansom, Colin Ward and many others.

£3.50 (including postage and packing)   ISBN 0 900384 66 2

Our full booklist is available from Freedom Press,
84b Whitechapel High Street, London E1 7QX or see our website at
www.freedompress.org.uk

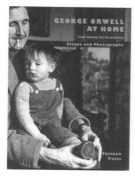

Freedom Press also publishes the anarchist
paper *Freedom*. For our current subscription
rates contact us at: Freedom Press,
84b Whitechapel High Street, London E1 7QX
or visit our website at
www.freedompress.org.uk